THROUGH THE CIRCLES OF HELL: A SOLDIER'S SAGA

Giuseppe Ciccone

THROUGH THE CIRCLES OF HELL: A SOLDIER'S SAGA

Giuseppe Ciccone

10 November 2016

Sandie Ville,

With best wishes,

J Richard Ciccone

Translated by
J. Richard Ciccone
Tina Ciccone Sturdevant

Illustrated by Philip Costa

Published by Relicum Press
ISBN: 978-0-692-42590-9
Printed by Blurb, Inc.
Printed in the United States
First published edition: March 2016

Unless otherwise stated, photographs are from the personal
collection of the translators.

The translators do not have control over and do not assume
any responsibility for author or third-party websites or their
content.

A portion of this book's proceeds will be donated to
organizations supporting Veterans.

Relicum Press

To my dear grandchildren
Maggie, Mary Liz, Tag, Vi and Zoe.
May understanding the past light the way to the future.
- JRC

To my children
Gary, Donna, Lisa and Linda. For the immeasurable love
and respect they show me every day.
- TCS

Contents

Contents

Acknowledgments

My deepest thanks to my wonderful wife, Natalie, for her support and her invaluable assistance in translating the poem and editing the text. I am grateful to our daughter Regina and her husband Stephen, our son Louis and his wife Nisha, and our son Robert and his wife Christine for their suggestions and encouragement.

I am indebted to Paolo Pollanzi for helping me better understand the World War I battlefield that was the Carso and assisting with the translation. Giovanni Traverso, Simona Traverso and Claudio Lenti also helped with the translation. Col. Rodolfo Sganga provided research of Italian military history and World War I.

My thanks to Philip Costa (CostaGrafix on Facebook) for his compelling illustrations. Jessica Mills and Ann Williams were conscientious typists and persevered through multiple drafts. My gratitude to Jaime Zigarowicz who transformed the manuscript into a book.

- JRC

The past is never dead.
It's not even past.

William Faulkner (*Requiem for a Nun*, 1951)

Preface
Tina Ciccone Sturdevant

Giuseppe Ciccone. Who was this man capable of writing such an incredible account of his experience as a soldier in the Italian Army during the Italy-Austria war? First and most important, he was my father. He was also a man of courage, honesty and integrity. He was a man who loved his family and a man who was very proud of his children. A man, who, even though he spent most of his life in America, loved his native country to the extent of making the supreme sacrifice of putting his life on the line in the defense of his beloved Italy. He was a self-educated man, as he demonstrated in his writing, but he must have had some knowledge of the classics, especially Dante's *Divine Comedy* as he makes metaphorical reference to it in various areas of his manuscript.

Giuseppe Ciccone was born on January 31, 1887 to Luigi Ciccone and Orsola Orlando in a small town named Sant'Eufemia d'Aspromonte in the province of Reggio Calabria, Italy. This village, which had a population of about six thousand citizens, is situated at the foot of the Aspromonte Mountains in the Calabria region of the southernmost part of the Italian peninsula. When he was four years of age, his mother died giving birth to a baby brother, Antonino. Later his father remarried a local lady name Fortunata Monterosso. Of their union, a son was born and they named him Domenico. Being the oldest of the three brothers, my father always felt a sense of responsibility toward his brothers even as adults and, at some point, he brought them to America with him.

I was told by my father's older sister, Francesca, that growing up, he developed into an intelligent and adventurous young man, dreaming that one day he would go to America. At the turn of the century, Italians viewed America as a land of young men's dreams. He was also influenced by an older cousin, Luigi Sinopoli, who had already found some success in the United States. The first of many trips to the United States, he left Sant'Eufemia with his cousin Luigi who acted as his unofficial guardian. They went to Naples, boarded a ship and began the 30-day voyage. They eventually settled in Auburn, New York.

In late 1916, my father returned to Italy to join the Army in the defense of his beloved country, which had entered the First World War in May 1915 as an ally of France and Great Britain. His manuscript tells the rest. His detailed account of his experience as a soldier in a war is one soldier's story. It could be any soldier's story for the fact that it tells us the tragedy of war and the pain and suffering of every soldier involved in direct combat. In addition, he gives us a view of the behavior of some misguided officers who were in charge but in reality did not possess the capacity to be leaders of men.

Among the many trips to the United States, one of the trips was made by necessity to save my father's life from the severe authority of the Fascist regime, the reign of terror that dominated Italy starting in 1925 when Benito Mussolini declared himself Dictator of Italy. I was told that my father was very critical of Mussolini. It was known that a knock at the door in the middle of the night was common for critics of the powerful Dictator. People were arrested, and some of them were never seen again. The family was afraid that it could happen to my father. A family meeting was held and it was decided that he would go to America. In the early fall of 1931, he boarded the local train in secrecy and escaped the Fascist tyranny.

In May 1971, accompanied by my husband Ernest Sturdevant and our four children, Gary, Donna, Lisa and Linda, I traveled to Italy to visit my parents, Giuseppe Ciccone and Francesca Maria Pillari. During that visit, my father gave me the manuscript. In recent years I began to reflect on the passage of this document to a new generation within the family. I chose to give it as a gift to my nephew,

Dr. J. Richard Ciccone. We've always called him Richard but the J stands for his given name of Joseph (Giuseppe in Italian).

My choice was made first of all because of my love and admiration for Richard and second because he is my father's first grandson. My nephew showed appreciation for the gift and helped me see that we possessed a good piece of literary work and a treasure trove of information. His enthusiasm complimented his knowledge of the First World War period. We set up a framework for the process of a translation and the work began. It was a joint effort and a pleasurable experience to work together. The original manuscript is written in Italian. Furthermore, it is written as poetry, which made it more challenging to translate into English. We knew from the beginning that it was imperative for us to maintain the integrity of the original text. Therefore, in order to achieve our objective, we read and discussed each and every line to assure that the translation would be true to the original text.

I loved my father and I felt his love for me but I did not know him well. By working on this document, I now have a greater understanding of his life and values, as well as his challenges.

My father, Giuseppe Ciccone–a self-educated man– left us a remarkable document. I find it difficult to express the extent of my gratitude to him as well as my admiration for his ability to write this detailed manuscript and to write it in poetic form.

Foreword
J. Richard Ciccone

He had a large, locked trunk that I knew nothing
about. He was quiet, detached, even distant from my point
of view. As a young boy of five or six, he was the
grandfather I knew existed but rarely saw. I was told that he
was going to give me a white horse for Christmas, the kind
ridden by the Lone Ranger. He never did. My cousin
Aurora, who lived with my grandfather for a time, reported
that he kept his bedroom door locked–the room where he
kept his large, locked trunk–not a trusting soul.

In September 2012, I visited my father's youngest
sister, Tina Ciccone Sturdevant at her home in Silver
Spring, Maryland. I was sitting at her kitchen table in the
middle of the afternoon when she excused herself. In a few
minutes she returned with a small composition notebook.
Her father, my grandfather, had given it to her many years
ago when she was in the midst of raising her four children
and developing her career. For reasons that she provides in
the preface, she decided to give it to me. Handing the
notebook to me, she said that she thought I would be
interested in it.

The document was written in Italian. With Tina's
help I began to read the first few lines and flipped through
the pages. Like Steinbeck exploring his hotel room in
Travels with Charlie, I searched different parts of the
material with no clear direction. I wanted to understand
what I was holding, reading, getting into. I noticed the
numbers, the comforting precision of numbers–54, 55, 56–
a number written at the top of each page. Written in his
distinctive handwriting, the manuscript began in the top
margin and went to the bottom of the page. Ten lines
between numbers. Why? Was this a poem? Was there a
rhyming scheme? There was: ab ab ab ab cc. This was not a
little story but a significant effort by a man with probably

xviii   Through the Circles of Hell: A Soldier's Saga

no more than a sixth grade education and a large, locked trunk. What had he been hiding? (1)
We sat reading, translating different passages, jumping ahead. Where was the saga going? He left to go to war, was seriously wounded and returned from battle quiet, detached and distant. At times Tina wept as we read and translated the text. It turned out that she did not know much more about him than I did. We exchanged what we knew or thought we knew about Nonno (Grandfather in Italian). Three hours later, with the arrival of my cousin Gary, Tina's son, we forced ourselves to stop for dinner.

I was determined to translate my grandfather's poetic saga. I eagerly jumped into the deep end. What hubris. I have limited knowledge of Italian and no experience as a poet except for some Billy Collins-like amusement. I was encouraged by Tina's eagerness to be involved in translating the poem. She proved to be a knowledgeable, thoughtful, patient collaborator.

By translating his poem, we hoped to give Nonno voice. Tina and I wanted to make every effort to be faithful to Nonno's poem and chose free verse as our medium. I also hoped to get to know this distant man. I discovered that he had a rich, active, vital inner life. It turned out that many of his interests (e.g., history, mythology, literature, politics and theology) overlapped with many of my interests. Who knew? Genetics, cultural influence, familial transmission are all powerful intergenerational ties.

How to translate from Italian to English? The rhyme scheme was similar to what Torquato Tasso, Italy's second greatest poet, used in *La Gerusalemme Liberata* (*Jerusalem Delivered*) in 1581, which he was best known for. He

---

(1) Nonna (Grandmother in Italian) Francesca Pillari Ciccone reported that he came home from the war a changed man: "Io parlavo di ceci, e lui parlava di favi [I was speaking about ceci beans and he spoke about fava beans]." He occasionally made statements that seemed to lack context. Nonna called these "lines in the air." (Tina Ciccone Sturdevant, personal communication, January 2013).

influenced a number of artists, poets and composers. In a list of great Italian poets, Tasso is second only to Dante. This classic was one of only three books that Tina remembered Nonno kept in the large, locked trunk. She recalled two other novels that he had in his trunk: Victor Hugo's *Les Miserables* and Alessandro Manzoni's *The Bethrothed*, a historical novel set in the 17th century. (2) These books each carry a message of Christian redemption. There were other books in the trunk, the titles of which are lost to us. It is not much of a guess to include Dante's *Divine Comedy*. We turned to translations of Dante's *Inferno* and studied 11 translations of Canto XIII. (3)

---

(2) Alessandro Manzoni was the grandson of Cesare Beccaria, the great Italian criminologist and champion of humanizing the criminal code.

(3) Translations of Dante Alighieri's *Divine Comedy: Inferno*
- a.　　John Ciardi *The Divine Comedy*
　　　　NY: W.W. Norton & Company, 1970
- b.　　Anthony Esolen *Inferno*
　　　　NY: The Modern Library, 2005 [1st edition 2003]
- c.　　Robert Hollander and Jean Hollander *The Inferno*
　　　　NY: Doubleday, 2000
- d.　　Clive James *The Divine Comedy*
　　　　NY: W.W. Norton & Company, 2013
- e.　　Henry Wadsworth Longellow *The Divine Comedy*
　　　　NY: Barnes and Noble, 2008 [completed between 1865 and 1867]
- f.　　Allen Mandelbaum *The Inferno*
　　　　Berkeley, CA: University of California Press, 1980
- g.　　Mark Musa *The Divine Comedy Volume I: Inferno*
　　　　NY: Penguin Books, 2003 [1st edition 1971]
- h.　　Michael Palma *The Inferno*
　　　　NY: W.W. Norton & Company, 2002
- i.　　Dorothy L. Sayers *The Divine Comedy 1: Hell*
　　　　London: Penguin Books, 1949
- j.　　Charles S. Singleton *The Divine Comedy – Inferno*
　　　　I.　　Italian Text and Translation
　　　　II.　　Commentary
　　　　Princeton, NJ: Princeton University Press, 1970
- k.　　Elio Zuppulla *The Inferno*
　　　　NY: Pantheon Books, 1998

It was clear that each translator, from Longfellow to Mandelbaum to Ciardi, brought their own voices to the words and music of Dante. The translation of Nonno's work would not be perfect but, no matter, who better to give voice to this silent man than his daughter and grandson.

The poem must have been written and rewritten a number of times before it was copied as a finished product into the composition notebook. (4) We do not know when the poem was written. We believe there were additional stanzas, probably copied into a second composition notebook that has been lost. The poem begins in November 1916 and comes to a halt in August 1917. Tina received the poem from her father in June 1972 when she and her family visited her hometown in Southern Italy, Sant'Eufemia d'Aspromonte. Our translation began in September 2012. To make our way through the epic poem, we scheduled many telephone meetings, usually one to two hours in length. We uncovered a number of historic, mythological, religious, philosophic and political references, some of which are discussed in the footnotes.

In his poem, Nonno does not dwell on descriptions of the landscapes, whether it be Sant'Eufemia d'Aspromonte or the battlefield of the Carso, located northwest of Trieste on the border with Slovenia. The difficulties of the terrain is trivial when compared to the treachery he encountered and his struggle to stay alive— getting enough to eat, escaping bombs and bullets. He uses simple language to convey complex concepts with glimpses into the inner life of one who read and, as far as we know, read alone without academic discussion of the concepts he encountered.

This firsthand account of becoming a soldier and going to war represents a microcosm of the universal soldier's experience. The poem focuses on a searing ember

---

(4) The cover's Cornell University logo is believed to predate the 1940s (Cornell University archivist, personal communication, October 2015).

of the hellish fire that was WWI: The battles on the Carso. The historian might provide a summary of the conditions (a blue, green mist covered the battlefield) while Nonno's account gives a report from within the chaos–"The battlefield was dark and very hot" (see Part 18: The Carso, page 103, line 9).

The story gets its strength from its simplicity and sincerity. A man returns to his native land to help defend it and finds corruption, injustice, propaganda and incompetent leadership on the battlefield. In the Tenth Battle of the Isonzo, he tells us that he relied on his intelligence and courage to survive. This is the only line in the poem where he engages in anything resembling self-praise (see Part 19: The Support Trench, page 101, line 1).

After a first draft of the translation, which took us months to complete, we had a list of more than 70 words and phrases that we did not understand and could not translate. As we learned more about World War I, the Italian-Austrian Front, the Battles of the Isonzo, the terrain of the Carso and trench warfare, we began understanding many of the words on our list. To add clarity to the narrative of the poem, we took the liberty of adding section headings.

Why did Giuseppe Ciccone (January 31, 1887 – March 31, 1975) decide to write this poem and quietly give it to his daughter, Tina, who decided in 2012 to bring it to light? I think the poem was the result of an unsuccessful effort to heal from the emotional wounds of war that we now call Post-Traumatic Stress Disorder (PTSD). During World War I the term in vogue was "shell shock"–a warrior's reaction to intense bombardment and battle.

As a psychiatrist, why do I think of PTSD? In the poem, my grandfather describes a series of traumatic events. On May 14, 1917, events 1-10 occurred during the Tenth Battle of the Isonzo. From May 14 to August 5, 1917, he continued to be traumatized after he was injured and left the battlefield, events 11-12.

1. The Austrian artillery was intensely shelling his regiment and he was expected to die (p. 85).

2. A shell exploded near him and buried him alive in the communication trench (p. 87).

3. He was saved by soldiers who dug him out but he sustained a severe leg (buttock) wound (p. 87).

4. Unable to walk, he crawled for help (p. 89).

5. He made his way through a field of death and destruction (p. 91).

6. As he tried to escape the chaos of the battlefield, he was hit by shell fragments and knocked unconscious (p. 93).

7. He awoke unable to see clearly (p. 95).

8. Asking for assistance, the officer of his unit threatened to shoot him (p. 95). This was no idle threat as it was widely known that Italian officers had executed their own soldiers on orders from General Luigi Cadorna.

9. Unable to walk, a soldier put him on his back. As they exited the tunnel, they found a massacre and the soldier threw him to the ground (p. 99).

10. He made his way to the field hospital (p. 103).

11. He was evacuated to a hospital behind the lines where he stayed for three months. There he was assaulted by the repeated howls of soldiers being "butchered"– having their limbs cut off (p. 107).

12. On August 7, 1917, he rejoined the Ferrara Brigade. It is likely that he fought in the Eleventh and Twelfth (Caporetto) Battles of the Isonzo (p. 113).

Jonathan Shay, MD, a psychiatrist, has written about the American soldier in Vietnam and PTSD. (5, 6) The unethical behavior by military officers–a betrayal of what was right–contributed to the catastrophic experience and, in Shay's view, led to their debilitating psychiatric symptoms of PTSD. (7) PTSD can devastate an individual's ability to live and participate in life (work and family). This withdrawal and emotional separation from others is amplified by the unethical, morally indefensible actions of military leaders.

After the unification of Italy in 1870, the North dominated the landscape. There was massive emigration from Southern Italy. Nonetheless, a large number of the Italian soldiers were from Southern Italy, some like Nonno returning from overseas to fight in WWI. Marching through northern Italian cities to the cheers of the populace, including the cheers of young men not required to serve, Nonno wrote, "Yes, you cheer but we are going to our deaths." This sense of doom coupled with inadequate training and materials and political and military leaders who were incompetent and "not doing the right thing" set the stage for his being nearly mortally wounded not once but a number of times, including sustaining a traumatic brain injury/concussion with loss of consciousness. For me, these provide more than enough ingredients to suggest he suffered from PTSD and explain some of his subsequent distant behavior.

Yet, this is only part of the story. What was he like prior to going into battle? We have scant information. We know his father, Luigi Ciccone, married Orsola Orlando

(5) Shay, Jonathan. *Achilles in Vietnam: Combat Trauma and the Undoing of Character.* New York: Simon & Schuster, 1995.

(6) Shay, Jonathan. *Odysseus in America: Combat Trauma and the Trials of Homecoming.* New York: Scriber, 2002.

(7) *Diagnostic and Statistical Manual of Mental Disorders, 5th Edition.* Virginia: American Psychiatric Association, 2013, pp. 265, 271-280.

xxiv   *Through the Circles of Hell: A Soldier's Saga*

and they had three children: Francesca, Giuseppe (Nonno) and Antonio. How did the death of his mother in childbirth when he was about four affect his view of the world and his repertoire for recovery? His father remarried and by all accounts his step-mother, Fortunata Monterosso, was kind. A half-brother, Domenico, was born of this union. In 1901, when he was fourteen he came to the United States with his older cousin Luigi Ciccone of Sinopoli. He visited his hometown of Sant'Eufemia in December 1908 when he was 21 and, while there, his step-mother died in a massive earthquake–not an easy adolescence and young adulthood.

In May 1912, Nonno married Francesca Pillari. They had five children, all born in Italy: Louis, Nino, Orsola, Rose and Tina. Like many Italian immigrants, Nonno worked in the United States and made periodic visits to his wife and family in Italy. My grandmother was one of a group of woman that Gay Talese described as "white widows," i.e., "the wives of ambitious young men who had left the village [at times absent for several years] to make money in America." (8)

However, what I do know points to the fact that the war forever changed him. Did he have PTSD? He locked his trunk, locked his room and locked himself from others. But in his trunk he had a world of books. In his room he wrote and rewrote, I think, in an effort to heal. In his head was a universe of ideas. His simple story is in many ways the universal story of soldiers throughout history, from the Trojan War, to the soldiers in Vietnam, Iraq and Afghanistan.

All too often, the focus is on the political leaders and generals. For example, the National Archeological Museum of Naples houses the Roman mosaic depicting the 331 B.C.E. battle between the Macedonian Alexander the Great and the Persian King Darius. Alexander and Darius take center stage in this historic narrative mosaic. The

---

(8) Talese, Gay. *Unto the Sons*. New York: Icnopf, 1992, p. 32.

fallen and fighting soldiers play a supporting role. In Nonno's poem, it is the archetypal soldier who takes center stage.

The feelings, the fears, the injuries of this World War I soldier transcend time and location and are universal. This poem, I believe, was his personal effort to connect with his wife and his children, his grandchildren and the world. I wish I could have spoken about all of this with him when visiting my grandparents in Sant'Eufemia in August 1973. The trunk was locked, as was the man, but I thank him for the gift of his poem.

Introduction
J. Richard Ciccone

*...the most colossal, murderous, mismanaged butchery that
has ever taken place on earth. Any writer who said
otherwise lied. So the writers either wrote propaganda,
shut up, or fought.*
Ernest Hemingway on World War I (quoted in Robert
Hughes' *The Shock of the New*, 1980)

Walk into World War I through the poetic words of
Giuseppe Ciccone, an Italian living in the United States
who heeds Italy's call to return to defend the motherland.
He faces the ravages of war as a member of Italy's Ferrara
Brigade with resolve, commitment and the understandable
human emotions of dread and fear, a constellation of
characteristics that can be defined as courage.

The catastrophe that was World War I can, in print,
be traced to the animosities of the royal families of Europe.
Queen Victoria was the British Monarch from 1837 until
her death in 1901. She married Prince Albert and their nine
children married into royal families of Europe. Her son
and successor, Edward VII, died in 1910. Barbara
Tuchman, in her masterful *The Guns of August*, opens with
a description of his funeral and the complicated kinships
and relationships among Europe's royal families. Tuchman
reminds the reader that Edward VII had been called the
"Uncle of Europe," not only uncle to Kaiser Wilhelm but
related directly or through marriage to the Czar of Russia,
and many of the royal families of Europe. A number of
members of this extended family did not get along. For
example, Edward VII and his nephew Kaiser Wilhelm
shared a mutual dislike of each other. At Edward VII's
funeral in 1910, Kaiser Wilhelm rode next to cousin
George V, the new king of England. By 1914, these cousins
would be at war.

Much has been written about World War I. This war

of attrition left Europe changed forever. If it did not kill, it wounded the West's sense of the promise of modernity, the inevitability of progress– progress in the standard of living, progress toward a more human society, progress toward a finer aesthetic. In Hew Strachan's *The Oxford Illustrated History of the First World War*, Modris Ekskin writes, "In its implosive and disintegrative power, the Great War...did have a positive side. By subverting context it liberated text. By undermining old authority, it rebased creativity. It threw us back upon ourselves. In that sense it was and remains the great emancipatory adventure– experience of the modern age, open to all, involving all, democratic, symbolic, and inescapable (p. 329)."

All this may be true but it was an avoidable, savagely destructive event that slaughtered millions, wounded millions more and infected the souls of many who survived. On the eastern front, Italy and Austria fought for a few miles of terrain. The number of casualties in WWI is not precise. Numbers cannot convey the individual tragedies, the families' grief for the dead, or the extent of the brutality on the survivors' psyches. The estimate of the overall casualties of WWI is 17 million deaths (10 million soldiers and seven million civilians) and 20 million wounded soldiers. Approximately 650,000 Italian soldiers were killed and another 950,000 were wounded. Malnutrition and disease led to the death of an estimated 590,000 Italian civilians. Total Italian deaths were approximately 1.1 million (about 3% of the population). About 1.4 million Austro-Hungarian soldiers were killed and another 3.6 million wounded. Malnutrition and disease led to the death of an estimated 600,000 Austro-Hungarian civilians. Total Austro-Hungarian deaths were 1.9 million (about 4% of the population).

The war between Italy and Austria was marked by the Twelve Battles of the Isonzo, named after the Isonzo River, located between Venice and Trieste. Battles One through Twelve took place between June 1915 and

November 1917. Giuseppe Ciccone, soldier/poet, participated in the Tenth Battle of the Isonzo and possibly the Eleventh and Twelfth Battles of the Isonzo. The Twelfth Battle of the Isonzo, the Battle of Caporetto, is the backdrop of Ernest Hemingway's *A Farewell to Arms.*

The Seventh, Eighth and Ninth battles of the Isonzo were focused on extending the Italian line east of Gorizia. The Tenth Battle of the Isonzo, which began on May 10, 1917 with preliminary artillery bombardment, was on the Carso (Karst) plain southeast of Gorizia with the goal of capturing Trieste. The Italians advanced as far as the town of Duino, about nine miles northwest of Trieste. This poem takes us to the Tenth Battle of the Isonzo (May 10, 1917 to June 8, 1917). In the Tenth Battle of the Isonzo, the Italians suffered 157,000 casualties and there were 75,000 Austro-Hungarian casualties.

The less than competent Italian Chief of Staff, General Luigi Cadorna, had commanded all ten of the unsuccessful Isonzo battles. Cadorna "chose to attribute his setbacks to apathy at home and cowardice among the army. Cadorna was brutal in his implementation of the military death penalty; he authorized the execution of over 750 men and routinely purged his senior commanders dismissing some 217 senior officers for perceived incompetence." (www.firstworldwar.com/bio/cadorna.htm)

After sustaining injuries requiring a three-month hospitalization, the soldier/poet rejoins his regiment and the Ferrara Brigade on August 5, 1917 in San Leonardo about 10 miles from the Bainsizza plateau and about 15 miles from Caporetto (Kobarid in the Slovenian language).

On August 19, 1917, two weeks after the poem leaves off, Cadorna ordered the Eleventh Battle of the Isonzo. This included an assault on the Bainsizza plateau (Banjška planota). The Eleventh Battle concludes on September 12, 1917. On September 23, 1917, the New York Times reported, "In the Bainsizza plateau the Austrians, after violent artillery preparations, repeatedly attacked the Italian positions...but were repulsed."

The Ferrara Brigade also fought in the Twelfth Battle of the Isonzo (The Battle of Caporetto, October 24, 1917 to November 12, 1917). In August 1917, the German Field marshall Von Hindenburg decided to support the Austro-Hungarian Army to rout the Italian Army. This he did by organizing a gas attack in the Caporetto area. On October 24, 1917 at 02:00 hours, almost 900 canisters of phosgene gas were fired at the Italian troops. They were buried in a fog of poison. Their gas masks were totally ineffective against phosgene. Between 500 and 800 Italian soldiers died within minutes. The approximately 200 survivors fled. A cascade of events weakened the entire Italian position and Cadorna was compelled to retreat, first to Tagliamento (about 25 miles southwest of Udine), and then to the Piave river. After Caporetto, Italian Chief of Staff General Cadorna from Piedmont was forced to resign. This is the context in which the soldier who wrote this poem served.

Maps

Map 1: Modern Italy

Map 2: Sant'Eufemia and surrounding towns

Map 3: Squinzano and the area of
Giuseppe Ciccone's basic training

Map 4: Giuseppe Ciccone's travel from basic training to the war front in northen Italy. The arrows shown indicate the course of his travel (see p. xxxiv for enlarged inset map of the area contained in the rectangular box).

Map 5: The location of the towns and notable mountains in or near the combat area (see p. xxxiii for geographic context).

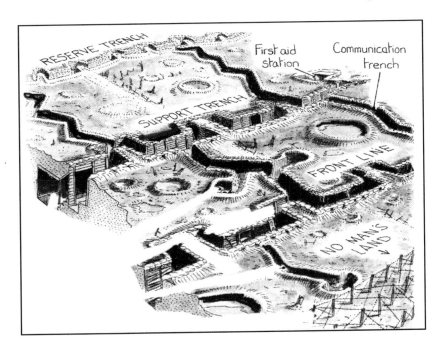

Map 6: A Theoretical Trench System

Trench warfare was not invented in World War I but in that conflict the trench evolved into a complex system of connected trenches with specialized functions. The Carso is a limestone plateau in which the warring Italian and Austro-Hungarian armies dug trenches. A number of them can be seen today at the World War I Memorial Park located a few miles north of Monfalcone, Italy (see pages 115-121 for photographs).

The schematic above depicts a theoretical trench system with front line, support, and reserve trenches connected by communciation trenches. Some sections of the trenches had specialized functions: Dugouts for cooking, eating and sleeping, latrines, and first aid.

The trenches were often eight to ten feet deep and four to six feet wide. A direct hit by a large artillery shell could collapse these limestone trenchs. Exploding artillery shells could also launch shards of limestone that wounded and killed soldiers.

Giuseppe Ciccone
(Year unknown)

The front cover of Giuseppe Ciccone's composition notebook

Guerra Italo Austriaca:
Storia Della Mia Vita Sventurata

Per un strano accidente
Parto dell'America adolorato
Era l'anno 16 cominciando il 1917
Per fare l'obrico di cittadino onorato
Per aiutare la Patria gloriosamente
Che mi spettava di diritto il soldato
Con me aveva due mie fratelli
Massimamente uno sfortunato
L'Austria per me fu la mia rovina
Barbara di cuore e assassina.
Parto da New York tutto penzoso
Navigando in alto mare
Il 21 Ottobre io era dubioso
Con male tempo che mi faceva male
Il vapore era grandioso
Il Duca D'Aosta si voleva chiamare
E una notte scura distintamente
Ebemo i primi tradimente.

Italian Austrian War:
The Story of My Unfortunate Life

The Odyssey Begins

By a twist of fate,
Near the end of 1916, approaching 1917,
I left America filled with anguish,
To do my duty as an honorable [Italian] citizen. (1)
To help my country to glory,
I was expected to fulfill my military obligation. (2)
My two brothers (3) were with me.
One was especially unfortunate. (4)
For me, going to war with Austria resulted in my total
    ruination.
Austrians have the barbarian hearts of assassins.

I left the port of New York in agitated, deep thought.
Navigating the high seas,
On the 21st of October, I was filled with apprehension.
The bad weather made me seasick.
The ship, which was very large,
Was called the Duca d'Aosta. (5)
It was on a distinctly dark night
That we were first betrayed.

---

(1) The rhetoric and slogans of World War I involving honor, sacrifice and "the war to end all wars" set the stage for soldiers to take to the battlefield. As Robert Hughes wrote, "To take up the sword and rush on winged feet to save civilization was one matter. To spend month after month sharing a rat-infested trench with other conscripts, driven half-crazy by the shelling…that was quite another. For the soldiers, there was no way of telling the truth about the war, except in private poetry." (Hughes, Robert. *The Shock of the New.* New York: Alfred A. Knopf, 1980, p. 58).

(2) During World War I, many Italian citizens living abroad were required to report for military service. Regio Decreto (Royal Decree) n. 1497 dated December 24, 1911. (Continued)

Il comandante del nostro vapore
Ebbe l'avviso lestamente
La nave Germanica fece telefone
Mi andiamo a salvare gli agente
Ma il nostro Capitano ci disse le contro parole
La nave nemica non spiego' niente
Allora noi pieni di terrore
Ci imaginammo i tradimente
E abbiamo piantato i nostri cannoni
In caso di battaglia contro i traditori
Sapete che paura miei care Signore
Che ebbemo sopra la nave
Di queste brigante e traditore
Che sono i Tedesche razze infame
Anno il veleno come I scorpioni
Per forza ci volevano afondare
Andava veloce il nostro vapore
Tempo due ore ci vennemo alontanare
E vennemo subito a scomparire
Ringraziando l'arcane Divine.

The Captain of the ship
Was advised via wireless telegraph (6)
That a German ship was in trouble
And needed our help to save its passengers.
But when our Captain asked for the password,
The enemy ship did not reply.
Now we were all terrorized.
We understood that we were being lured into a trap.
So we prepared our cannons
For a potential battle against the deceivers.

Imagine the fear, my dear people,
That engulfed our ship.
Murderers and traitors,
These Germans are a race of despicable people.
They are like scorpions full of poison.
They were determined to sink our ship.
We sped away.
After two hours, we distanced ourselves from them
And we felt safe for the moment
Thanks to the inscrutable Divine.

(2)...If they failed to report, they were declared "renitente [reluctant]" and subject to punishment (Article 144). They could be sentenced to one to two years of imprisonment. During wartime, the punishment could be doubled. (Col. Rodolfo Sganga, Italian Military Attaché, Italian Embassy, personal communication, June 12, 2015).

(3) Antonino (Anthony) [mother- Orsola Orlando] and Domenico (Dominick) [half-brother- mother Fortunata Monterosso].

(4) Antonio's wife Teresa suffered from a significant mental illness. They had no children. Luigi Pirandello, winner of the Nobel Prize in Literature, was married to Antoinette Portulano who also suffered from a significant psychotic illness. Pirandello's plays and novels provide insight into the profound impact of living with an individual with a psychotic illness.

(5) The S.S. Duca d'Aosta, an Italian oceanliner, was launched in 1908. In May 1918, it was chartered to carry U.S. troops to Brest, France. It was 475-feet-long and 53-feet abeam. (Continued)

Dopo un paio di giorni vennemo a scoprire
Le terre d'Europa alegramente
Piccole e grande venite a sentire
Che contentezza per tutte gli agente
Io ero contento non si puo' dire
Avevamo scanzate le tradimente
Ormai eramo nelle terre vicine
Eramo lontane di quelli insolente
Finalmente vittimo terra
Ecco lo Stretto di Gibilterra
Giorno 2 Novembre costigiamo la Sardegna
Arivava la nave dei militare
Dopo un giorno arivamo a Genova
Tutte le borghese si mesero a gridare
Arivamo tutte nella nostra terra
Nei nostre terre Italiane
Evvero che andavamo tutte in guerra
La Patria andavamo aiutare
Ariva alla banchina il nostro vapore
E alzano la nostra Bandiera il tre colore
Ci guardano tutte con buona vista
Ecco le soldate riselvista.

Return and Corruption

Happily, after a few days,
We saw land. We saw Europe.
Young and old alike, come and hear about
The joy felt by all on board the ship.
I cannot express how happy I was that
We were now near land.
We had escaped the treachery.
And were far from the shameless German ship.
At last, we could see land and
The Straits of Gibraltar.

On the second of November [1916], we sailed along the
    coast of Sardinia. (7)
The ship with the soldiers was arriving.
The next day we docked in Genoa,
Where the people welcomed us with cheers.
We had all arrived at our homeland,
To our beloved Italy.
It is true; we were all going to war.
We were going to help our motherland.
Our ship arrived at the dock
And we raised our Italian flag, the tricolor.
They looked at us with pride and said,
"Here are the Reserve Soldiers."

---

(5)...The S.S. Duca d'Aosta could carry 80 first-class, 16 second-class
and 1,740 third-class passengers. It often sailed from New York to
Genoa. It appears that, at some point, it was equipped with cannons.

(6) Guglielmo Marconi, the Italian inventor and Nobel Prize winner in
Physics, patented a wireless telegraphy system in 1897. Most wireless
telegraphy communications used Morse code.

(7) The Island of Sardinia is slightly smaller than Sicily. It has evidence
of Paleolithic colonization and 7,000 very interesting stone structures
called nuraghes. The nuraghes were constructed between 1900 and 730
B.C.E. and are the symbol of Sardinia. (Continued)

A Genova vennemo a sbarcare
Il 3 Novembre con confusione
Come le soldate ci misero a marciare
Alla Dogana miei care signore
Le casse dovevamo daziare
Con molte grida della popolazione
Sono arivate le militare
Non anno paura dei cannone
Vennero delle terre americane
Contro Cecco Peppe and Gugliolmone
E ci passano tutte a fila
Quando mi disbrigai fame sentiva
Un Napoletano si e' presentato
Gli oggetti miei deve passare
Le valigie a passata
Ma delle casse niente vozze fare
La sera innanze a me si e' invicinato
Che lire 20 doveva pagare
Io ci disse tu non ai fatto il tuo dovere
Per mio onore ti dono 3 lire

On the third of November, with confusion,
We disembarked in Genoa.
Then, we began to march like soldiers.
We had to go through customs, my dear friends,
Where we had to pay the duty fee.
The populace was cheering,
"The soldiers have arrived.
They are not afraid of the cannons.
They came from America
To fight Frankie-Joey and Willie." (8)
After we marched past them in a line,
I realized I was hungry.

As we paused in formation,
I was confronted by a Neapolitan Customs Agent.
My things had to go through customs.
The suitcases passed customs
But the Neapolitan did not want to deal with my trunk.
That evening the Neapolitan customs agent approached me
Saying that I would have to pay him 20 Lire.
I told him, "You did not do your job.
But out of the goodness of my heart, I will give you three
    lire."

(7)...Defensive structures, they were part of the Nuragic civilization
that some scholars have described as the most advanced civilization in
the western Mediterranean at the time. A number of them are World
Heritage Sites. In 1847, Sardinia entered into a union with Piedmont
under the House of Savoy, which played an important role in the
unification of Italy. The unification was completed in 1871 when Rome
became the capital of the kingdom of Italy. Garibaldi spent the last
years of his life in Caprera, Sardinia.

(8) "Frankie-Joey" is Emperor Franz Joseph I (b. August 18, 1830;
d. November 21, 1916). "Willie" is Kaiser Wilhelm II (b. January 27,
1859; d. June 4, 1941).

Franz Joseph I was Emperor of the Austro-Hungarian Empire from
1848 until his death. His nephew Archduke Franz Ferdinand was
assassinated on June 28, 1848 in Sarajevo, Bosnia. (Continued)

Quello Napoletano si viene a imbestialire
Dicendo che non lo pagava onestamente
Io mi infurio come una tighe
Dicendo vai via prepotente
Piccole e grande venite a sentire
Che uomo infame e strafotente
Ci disse non ti voglio piu' vedere
Tu non ai fatto niente
Male parole ci vozze dire
Mi ai fatto perdere le senze
E ci disse cose belle
Ti lascio che ci sono i miei fratelli
Partimo subito per la stazione
Si spetta il treno alle 9 per partire
Viene alle 11 con molto rumore
Come il vento ci fece spedire
Il diretto era con molto terrore
Andava veloce non si puo' dire
In prima classe mi segnaro la vettura
Silenzio anno fatto le conditura

The Neapolitan began to curse me
Saying that I did not pay him fairly.
I became as furious as a tiger
And said, "Go away you bully."
Young and old alike come and hear me.
I told this outrageous and arrogant man,
"I do not want to see you anymore.
You did not do anything for me."
I wanted to tell him even more
Because he made me lose my temper
I told him a thing or two
But I let it go because my two brothers were nearby.

On to Sant'Eufemia d'Aspromonte (9)

We left quickly for the train station
To catch the nine a.m. train,
The train arrived at eleven a.m., with much noise.
Moving as fast as the wind,
The express train traveled with a great roar.
It is hard to describe how fast it was going.
They assigned me to a seat in the first class car.
The conductors told us to keep silent.

---

(8)...The Archduke was riding in an open car when a Serbian nationalist threw a bomb at him. The bomb wounded an officer and some of the crowd. That afternoon, driving to visit the wounded officer, the Archduke's driver made a wrong turn. The car happened to pass by another Serbian nationalist, Gavrilo Princip, who used this unexpected opportunity to shoot and mortally wound the Archduke and his wife. This started a cascade of events that led to World War I. Austria-Hungary declared war on Serbia on July 28, 1914. Within days Austria-Hungry and Germany were allied against Russia, France and Great Britain.

Kaiser Wilhelm II was the firstborn grandchild of Queen Victoria. He became the Kaiser of Germany in 1888. His accountability for the start of World War I and the part he played in Germany's war tactics are controversial. He abdicated in November 1918 and went to the Netherlands in exile.

Io partiva con troppo premura
Che il treno veneva a solicitare
Alle 11 di sera eravamo a Roma
Alle 4 Novembre si vennero a fare
Era stanca la mia persona
Solicitamo presto a mangiare
A mezzo a persone infamuna
Con le miei fratelli venne a stare
Cerano Officiale di tutte le Nazione
Arabi, Africane e del Giappone
Io ringrio l'eterno Dio
Lasciai l'abergo e me ne andava
Pure le miei fratelli e anche io
E a Roma io la salutava
Il treno vozze pigliare io
Che nella Calabria andava
Partimmo il treno scompario
Di Roma mi allontanava
Cerano soldati pure Inglesi
Russe, Americane pure Francese.

I was so eager to get home
That I wished the train would go even faster.
At eleven at night we arrived in Rome.
It was almost November fourth.
I was very tired.
We quickly requested something to eat.
I was with my brothers and
We found ourselves in the midst of some obnoxious people,
Officers from various nations:
Arabs, Africans and Japanese.

Thanking the eternal Lord
I left the hotel
With my brothers
And said goodbye to Rome.
I wanted to catch the train
That was headed for Calabria.
We got on board and the train pulled out of the station.
We were putting Rome behind us.
On the train, there were soldiers from England,
Russia, America and even France.

---

(9) Sant'Eufemia d'Aspromonte is a town in the Province of Reggio Calabria. It is about 28 miles northeast of Reggio Calabria. In the last third of the 19th century and first half of the 20th century, the population of Sant'Eufemia hovered at approximately 6,000 inhabitants. Nonno's love for and pride in his hometown is evident in a brief history that he wrote about of Sant'Eufemia d'Aspromonte. He stated that the town may be of Greek origins.

The center of the town was once known as Mitra. The virgin and martyr Sant'Eufemia was from Chalcedon, located across the Bosporus strait from Byzantium (Constantinople/Istanbul).

Nonno wrote that the inhabitants of Sant'Eufemia have a long history of love of liberty and endured punishments as a result of their efforts to overturn the domination of others, e.g., the Count of Sinopoli and the Bourbons. In 1862, on his way to capture Rome and unify Italy, Garibaldi passed through the area of Sant'Eufemia. Nonna Francesca Pillari's grandfather and other townsmen joined Garibaldi's forces. (Continued)

A me mi scusate miei care amice
Il treno venne arivare
Mancava di tre anni e piu' mese
Il 5 novembre venne a scurare
Che doveva arivare al mio paese
Ad abracciare alle miei care
Io che lo dico mi venne le rise
La moglia mia dovevo abbracciare
Giorno 6 novembre a Napoli arrivamo
E due ore la' aspettamo
Dopo due ore mi mise a salire
Con le miei fratelli tutte a canto
La cerano le nostre serile
Il treno si infuria come il lampo
Scappava di certo non si puo' dire
Ed io sopra il treno sempre penzando
Che tutto al mondo ci sono destine
Il destino penzava mormorando
Che andava in guerra per morire
Dopo 22 ore il treno arivava
Ecco la citta' di Bagnara.

Forgive me my dear friends for my emotion,
I was going home.
I had been away for three years and some months.
It was the evening of the fifth of November.
I was on my way to my hometown
To embrace my loved ones,
To hug my wife.
I can tell you, a smile came to my face.
On the sixth of November, we arrived in Naples,
Where we waited for two hours.

After two hours, I re-boarded the train
With my brothers at my side.
We found our seats and
The train left like a bolt of lightning.
Certainly it was going faster than I can tell you.
I was on the train thinking,
For everything in the world there is a destiny.
I murmured to myself, "My destiny
Is to go to war and die."

————————————

(9)...Garibaldi, the Lion of Caprera, was wounded in Aspromonte. The
pine tree against which he leaned after being wounded is a historic site
and, for Nonno, a sacred place of pilgrimage that all who traveled to
Sant'Eufemia to see him were obliged to visit.

Arivando a Bagnara vozze fermare
Sono arivato alle 3 dopo mezza notte
Alle 7 Novembre si veniva a fare
Bagnara e' a mezzo alle monte
Alle parente venivo aspettare
Pensava la guerra e tante morte
Considerava le cose torte
Dopo 3 ore vedo alle miei parente
Vedo a mio figlio e a mia moglie
E disse io con molte stente
A tutte io abbracciava
Che nella miei terre arrivava
Alla abergo vozzimo andare
Io e anche le mie fratelli
Tutte quante andamo a mangiare
Col molto affanno e molte stenti
Non piu' pensavo le cose male
Ero contente allegramente
Mi sono allegrato di troppo vino
Ora il mio paese era vicino

After 22 hours, the train approached
The city of Bagnara. (10)
Arriving in Bagnara, we stopped.
We got there at three in the morning
On the seventh of November.
Bagnara, located on the sea, is surrounded by mountains.
Waiting for my relatives,
I thought of war, with all its deaths
And many horrors.

After three hours, I saw my relatives.
I saw my son and my wife.
Choking with emotion, I said,
"I hug all of you."
I had arrived in my native land
Along with my brothers.
We wanted to go to the restaurant
And everyone came with us to eat and celebrate.
Short of breath and speechless,
I was no longer filled with negative thoughts.
I was elated. My joy increased with the help of too much
        wine.
Finally, my hometown was near.

---

(10) Bagnara is a town in the Province of Reggio Calabria. It is located
on the Tyrrhenian Sea about 19 miles northeast of Reggio Calabria and
eight miles west of Sant'Eufemia d'Aspromonte.

Dopo mezzogiorno tutte partimo
Per la strata del nostro paese
Ci voleva due ore di camino
Mancava di tante anne e piu' mese
Con la amice mi ci vidimo
Da lontano vedo il mio paese
Venne un tempo che non voleva scampare
Pioveva forte e non poteva caminare
Sono arivato alla Citta' mia
Il bel paese di Santa Femia
Io penzava con molta dia
Che fra giorni doveva parire
La notte penzava e non dormia
E il penzero non mi faceva dormire
E penzava la moglie mia
Di giorno e giorno si doveva partire
Il figlio penzava e la sfortuna mia
Che doveva andare per morire
Quando il giorno 19 Dicembre
Occominciaro le prime tormente

It was noon when we left Bagnara.
And got on the road to Sant'Eufemia.
It was a two-hour walk.
I had been away several years and some months.
I was going to see my friends again
In the distance, I could see my hometown.
We were caught in a downpour with no letup.
It rained so hard that it was difficult to walk.
Finally, I arrived at my hometown,
The beautiful town of Sant'Eufemia

Treachery

At night, I was preoccupied and could not sleep.
I was thinking, with much foreboding,
That in a few days I would have to leave.
My fears kept me awake.
I was thinking of my wife.
In a few days, I would have to leave her.
I was thinking of my son and my destiny.
I was leaving to go to die.
On the 19th of December,
My torments began.

Del maresciallo mi viene la chiamata
Che doveva andare al mio Distretto
Lora mia era sonata
Giorno 20 mi trovai a Reggio
Penzava la mia vita sventurata
Tanto patire e molto tormento
La famiglia tutta adolorata
Con molte lagrime e lamento
A Reggio cera la confusione
Molte soldate e gran popolazione
Con me cerano le miei fratelli
Allora a casa me ne vozze scappare
Il treno da lontano presto si sente
Andavamo a fare le Feste di Natale
Perche' non si sapeva piu' l'anno venente
Dove lo veniva a fare
Vado a trovare a tutte le parente
Chi sa se ne vedemo piu'e ci vennemo abbracciare
Allora un paio di giorni mi so voluto stare
Mi finiscono le feste tutte pare.

I received a message from the Chief of Police (11)
That I had to report to the recruiting office.
My hour had arrived.
On the 20th of December I went to Reggio (12)
Thinking about my wretched life
That was filled with suffering and torment.
My family was grieving.
There were many tears and much loud wailing.
In Reggio, we found confusion,
With many soldiers and a teeming populace.

My brothers were with me.
From a distance we heard the train and
We decided to return home.
We wanted to celebrate Christmas at home.
Who knew where we would be next Christmas
Or, in fact, if we would be alive.
I went to see all my relatives.
We did not know if we would see each other ever again.
We embraced. After Christmas, we decided to stay a few
    more days
To complete the celebration of the Christmas season.

---

(11) In Italy there are both local and national police forces. The local
police include the Municipal Police (MP) and are usually found in large
cities. Among the national police forces is the Carabinieri, the national
military police of Italy with both military and civilian jurisdictions.
The Carabinieri were the local police force in Sant'Eufemia.

(12) Reggio Calabria is located at the toe of the Italian Peninsula where
the Aspromonte Mountains go down to the strait of Messina (across the
strait is Sicily and Messina). Its history dates back to 1500 B.C.E.
Named Rhegion when it was a Greek city, since Italian unification it
has been called Reggio di Calabria. Reggio Calabria has a beautiful
mile-long promenade along the coast (Lungomare). The Riace bronze
statues are housed in Reggio's Magna Grecian National Museum.

The region of Reggio is subject to major earthquakes. 25 percent of the
inhabitants of Reggio died in the earthquake of December 28, 1908.
(Continued)

Il maresciallo imietamente
Mi ha voluto domandare
Io ci disse rabiosamente
A Reggio non mi vozzero accettare
Che ci vonno i documente
E la non poteva stare
Domane viene subitamente
Che di tutto penzo io mi puoi stare
Ora io tutto comprendo
Vuoi il foglio di riconoscimento
Allora io con molto stento
Ci disse alle miei fratelli
Partimo che ora e' tempo
Mi licenzio con tutte le miei parente
Bacio la moglie e figlio e mi licenzio
Che doveva andare nel fuoco ardente
Venivano le pene del inferno
In ultimo disse non e' niente
La Patria mi viene a chiamare
Abbasso gli assassine e pure le infame

The Chief of Police of Sant' Eufemia saw that I had
    returned
He immediately asked me, "Why are you back?"
I angrily responded,
"They would not accept me in Reggio.
They wanted certain documents that I did not have
And I could not stay there."
He said, "Now I understand the problem.
Come to my office in the morning,
I will take care of everything. You will be able to stay in
    Reggio.
Do you want identification papers?"

And I, with much difficulty,
Told my brothers,
"The time has come for us to depart."
Once again, I took leave of my relatives.
Kissing my wife and son, I said my goodbyes.
I had to enter the infernal flames,
The pains of hell were coming.
Ultimately I said to my family, "It is nothing.
My country is calling me
To defeat the assassins and the infamous."

---

(12)...Messina was even more devastated; 40% of the inhabitants
perished in this earthquake. Sant'Eufemia felt the force of the quake.
Nonno was visiting Sant'Eufemia at the time. His stepmother was
killed by this earthquake. Rubble from this earthquake was still evident
in the early 1970s.

Nel mio paese cerano molte ruffiane
Con le miei fratelli andamo a Distretto
Sono spia certe paesane
Ci dissero a Distretto
A casa ancora vi potete stare
Io ci disse con molto stento
Sono state le infame
Del mio paese con tormamento
Le tuoi carte non si venno a trovare
Vai a Palmi in quel Distretto
Allora io e un fratello
Reggio vozzemo a lasciare
E quel altro mio fratello
Le carte vennero a trovare
Ci dissero loro fai presto
A Messina deve andare
La cera un bel Coronnello
A casa lo vozze mandare
Lo vedo a casa a notte scura
Alla faccia dei infame e carognuna

In my town there were many evil people.
With my brothers, I went to the district office [in Reggio].
At the district office, I told them,
"Some of my townsmen are informants." (13)
They said, "You can be at home for a few more days."
I told them, with much distress,
"There are detestable people
In my town who torment us."
They told me, "We cannot find your paperwork.
Go to the district office in Palmi." (14)

So I and one of my brothers [Domenico]
Left Reggio [and made our way back to Sant'Eufemia].
My other brother [Antonio],
Whose papers they had found,
Was told to leave immediately
To report to the district office in Messina. (15)
He reported to a kind Colonel
Who sent him home to Sant'Eufemia.
He arrived home in the darkness of night,
Thumbing his nose at the corrupt, contemptible informants.

---

(13) By "informants," Nonno is referring to townspeople who
functioned as spies. They made reports to the police (some accurate,
some not) perhaps to gain favor with the police/authorities. Using
citizens to spy on one another is not a recent innovation and continues
in modern times. Citizens in the Czech Republic and Romania have
told me (JRC) of the prevalence and perniciousness of "informants"
while they lived under communist regimes.

(14) Palmi is a town in Calabria. In 1910, it had a population of about
14,000 inhabitants. It is located on the coast of the Tyrrhenian Sea, 12
miles northwest of Sant'Eufemia d'Aspromonte.

(15) Messina is on the eastern shore of Sicily on the Strait of Messina.
Reggio Calabria is located on the opposite shore. The Strait of Messina
has a natural whirlpool that appears to be related to the myth of Scylla
and Charybdis. The two Greek mythological sea monsters lived on
opposite sides of the Strait of Messina. Charybdis was a sea nymph
who Zeus turned into a whirlpool that lethally swirled on one side of
the Strait of Messina. (Continued)

Mio fratello aveva il mandato di cattura
Le sbirre avezzero aspettare
Questa fu per loro una fortuna
A mio fratello mi puonno arrestare
Il maresciallo venne con una cagiuna
A casa mia a domandare
Disse tuo fratello dove a questa ora
E' a letto a riposare
Disse lui si chiama Antonio Ciccone
Voglio certe cose domandare
Ci disse io che andate cercando
Forse volete a me interogare
A tuo fratello vado trovando
Lui e' malato e a letto stave
Disse l'infame marasciallo
Una parola ci volevo spiare
Mi viene con me mi ci domando
A mio fratello doveva aresatare
Per la miseria di 14 lire
Lo bacio di Giuda fece quel vile.

There was a warrant for my brother's arrest.
The police were waiting.
It was a lucky break for them.
Because my brother was back in Sant'Eufemia,
They could arrest him easily.
The Chief of Police came to the house
With an excuse, inquiring,
"Where is your brother at this hour?"
"He is he in bed resting."
He said, "Is his name Antonio Ciccone?
I want to ask him a few questions."

I asked him, "What are you looking for?
Maybe you want to interrogate me?"
"I am looking for your brother."
"He is sick and he is in bed."
The vicious Chief of Police said,
"I just want to ask him a question."
"Come with me and I will ask him."
He was going to arrest my brother
For 14 miserable lire.
A coward had given the kiss of Judas.

---

(15)...Scylla was a sea nymph who Poseidon's jealous wife turned into a beast that barked like a dog. Scylla had twelve feet, six long heads and six mouths each with three rows of sharp teeth. She would grab and eat passing sailors. Odysseus' problems dealing with the two perils were chronicled in Homer's *The Odyssey* (Book XII).

La notte io non dormivo
Lui aveva paura che lo voleva sparare
Quello infame e assassino
Per 14 lire lo vozze arestare
Sapete che fece quel vile
Al carcere lo vozze portare
Mio fratello si mise a bramare
Dicendo carognoni e assassine
Questo e' l'onore si mise a gridare
Carognone assassine e infame
Malato era e si mise a pregare
Con tradimento lo vozzero chiudere
L'oro rispondono le infami
Ti abiamo arestato per 22 lire
Ci dissero 5 mese deve contare
La Guerra libica non venisti a servire
E percio' ti vennemo arestare
Questo e' certo e te lo volemo dire
Ordine ebbemo del tribonale
Di 15 giorni dietro ti dovevamo apresentare

That night I could not sleep.
My brother was afraid that they wanted to shoot him.
Those detestable villains
Wanted to arrest my brother for 14 lire.
Do you know what that low-life wanted to do?
He wanted to bring my brother to jail.
My brother confronted them,
Called them cowards and assassins.
"This is justice?" he began screaming
"Cowards, thugs and scoundrels."

He was sick and he began to pray.
As a result of treachery they imprisoned him.
The disgraceful cops said,
"We are arresting you for 22 lire." (16)
They told him, "You will have to spend five months in jail
Because you did not return to Italy to serve in the Libyan
          War. (17)
That is why we are arresting you.
This is certain and we want to inform you that
We have a court order,
Issued 15 days ago, to detain you." (18)

---

(16) There is an inconsistency with earlier accounts of the amount of the fine: 14 lire and 22 lire.

(17) The Libyan War (Italo-Turkish War) was fought between Italy and the Ottoman Empire from September 1911 to October 1912. Italy captured territory that became known as Italian Libya. Italy's relatively easy defeat of the Ottoman's forces encouraged Balkan nationalism.

(18) Antonio was arrested under the inquisitorial system, which was widely used in Europe in the 19th and much of the 20th century. In the inquisitorial system, the judge's role is to discover the facts while representing the interests of the state. The criminal defendant is not presumed guilty but neither is the criminal defendant presumed innocent. The assumption was that charges would not have been brought if there was not strong evidence against the defendant. Hence, there appears to be a not very subtle tone that the criminal defendant is guilty until proven innocent in the inquisitorial system.

Siete carogna e pure infame
E nella facce ve lo voglio dire
Col tradimente mi venistovo arestare
Con voi altre sbirre si mangia e si beve
Un uomo onesto sempre lo venite arestare
E con voi altre non si puo' dormire
A mio fratello lo vennero a interogare
Dicendo che mi volete dire
Lavocato disse puoi bene parlare
Per quale motivo ti portaro ccane
Mio fratello disse sono i destine
Col tradimento mi vozzero arestare
Sentite tutte il mio dire
5 mesi e mezzo devo scontare
Perche' la Patria non vennero a servire
5 anni dietro che vennero a passare
La Guerra libica vi voglio dire
Sono malato e non ho che fare
Nocente sono tutto noioso
In questo misero carcere e rinchiuso

My brother said, "You are cowards and thugs.
I want to tell you to your face.
Because of treachery, you came to arrest me.
People like you want to appear friendly
But you always arrest the honest man.
You are not to be trusted."
At the jail, they interrogated my brother,
Asking, "What do you want to tell me?"
The prosecutor said, "You can speak freely.
For what reason did they bring you to jail?"

My brother said, "It is the fates.
They arrested me as a result of a betrayal.
Listen everyone to what I have to say.
I have to serve five and a half months
Because I did not come back to serve my country.
Five years have passed
Since the war in Libya.
I am sick and there is nothing I can do.
I am innocent victim and I am exasperated
In this miserable cage-like jail."

Apresso giorno io vozze partire
Andare a Palmi al comandatore
Signore avvocato ci vozze dire
Mio fratello e' chiuso nella prigione
5 mesi di carcere deve finire
Per causa dell'infame e carognone
Lui disse ci vonno 300 lire
Tempo tre giorni tuo fratello e' fuori
Fece una suprica alle soprane
Che lo venero a liberare
Questo cose sono cose strane
Per mezzo del avocato
Fim[m]ano veneva chiamato
Che a me mi venne ad aiutare
Del mio paese lui era nato
Ed era nostri paesane
Io doveva partire per soldato
Ora che mio fratello venne a liberare
Mi venne il tempo di licenziare
A Reggio Calabria doveva andare

The next day, I went
To Palmi to see a senior criminal defense attorney
"Dear attorney, I want to tell you,
That my brother is locked in prison
And he has to serve five months
As a result of treachery and lies."
The lawyer said to me, "For 300 lire,
Within three days, your brother will be a free man.
I will petition the Court
Asking them to release him."

These things are hard to understand.
My brother was freed as a result of the intervention of the
        attorney,
Fimmano was his name.
He who was there to help us,
Was born in our hometown;
He was our townsman.
Now that my brother was free,
I had to leave to report to the army.
I just had time to say goodbye
I had to go to Reggio Calabria.

Da Reggio mi anno telegrafato
Che per distretto doveva partire
Subito sono arivato
Mi dissero a quale parte volete iri
Mi anno subito misurato
Un altro poco il paese lo voglio vedere
Signor Capitano ci ho domandato
Questo e' lo certe e ve lo voglio dire
5 giorni di licenza mi ha dato
Un'altra volta alle miei ho abracciato
Alle 25 Gennaio mi venne a distaccare
Partivo per Reggio con gran sudore
Il capitano era disturbato
Con l'occhi rosse e incazzato
Per voi altre ci voresse la prigione
Venistovo con un giorno di ritardo
Per questa volta io vi perdono
Fate il vostro dovere che ce' la disciplina
Era venuta ora la mia rovina

Reporting for Duty

I received a telegram from Reggio.
I was ordered to report to the recruiting office
And I arrived without delay.
They asked me where I would like to be assigned.
They quickly measured me for a uniform.
I said to the Captain,
"I would like to remain home for a little while longer."
This is certain and I want you to know,
He gave me five days of leave.
Once again I embraced my loved ones.

On January 25th [1917] the time had come for me to
    depart.
I was concerned as I left for Reggio.
The Captain was irate.
With fury in his eyes,
He angrily said,
"All of you should be in jail.
You returned one day late.
This time I am going to pardon you.
Do your duty from now on. Here in the army, there is
    discipline."
The hour of my ruin was at hand. (19)

---

(19) This phrase (one of many allusions to the New Testament that can be found in the poem) echoes words found in: (1) John 13:11 "Before the feast of Passover, Jesus, knowing that hour had come for him to pass out of this world..."; and (2) John 17:1 "Father, the hour has come!" (Saint Joseph Edition. *The New American Bible*. New York: Catholic Book Publishing Company, 1986).

Allora come e' venuta la sera
Mi domandaro il mio Reggimento
Volete andare per Messina
Al 6° Fanteria siete contento
Io ci disse con voce fina
Un giorno di licenza e sto attento
Il Capitano adiventa una tigra
Disse partite imiatamente
Io ci disse quanto siete bello
Mandatemi dove e' mio fratello
Subito mi dissero a dove stave
Io ci disse al Reggimento 47
La voi volete andare
Il Reggimento e' a Lecce
Subito mi mise allegrare
Andava alle gueri e patimente
Speranza di casa non ci stava
Ora accominciano i miei tormente
Io ho voluto e mi devo conortare
E' colpa mia mi faccio il militare

So as evening arrived,
I asked for the name of my regiment.
"You must go to Messina
To join the 6th Infantry. Are you happy?"
I told him in a whisper,
"Give me one more day of leave, and I will promptly
    return."
The Captain became as infuriated as a tiger
And said, "Leave immediately [for Messina]."
I told him, "Aren't you the gracious one?
Send me to my brother's regiment."

Quickly he replied, "Where is your brother?"
I responded, "With the 47th Regiment."
"You want to go there?
"That regiment is in Lecce." (20)
I was overjoyed [to be sent to the 47th Regiment].
I was going to war and misery.
There was no hope of my going home.
Now began my agony. (21)
I agreed to join the army and I must accept
That it is my fault that I am a soldier.

---

(20) The town of Lecce is the capital of the province of Lecce. It is in the heel of the boot of the Italian Peninsula, 300 miles from Reggio Calabria. Because of its Baroque architecture, it has been dubbed "The Florence of the South."

(21) This line evokes the Agony in the Garden: Luke 22:44 "He was in such agony and he prayed so fervently that his sweat became like drops of blood falling on the ground." (Saint Joseph Edition. *The New American Bible*. New York: Catholic Book Publishing Company, 1986).

Io niente ho voluto piu' sentire
Io era con un altro compagno
Il treno era pronto per partire
Erano le 8 avanzando
Certe volte sono le destine
E sopra il treno penzava tanto
Di Bovolino mi ha voluto dire
Di tante cose noi parlammo
Fino a Taranto insieme vozzemo iri
E dopo ci distaccammo
La citta di Taranto avemo arivato
E misono a dividire
Allora io era disturbato
Il treno era pronto per partire
Di Lecce il treno era pronto per partire
A Brindisi sono arivato
Le cose storte li venne a vedere
Certe soldate erano pure a lato
Dissero qui non fai come era la borghesia
Deve fare il soldato con energia

I did not want to hear anything else.
I was with another soldier.
The train was ready to leave.
It was a little after eight.
On the train, I was preoccupied and thought
How at times it is just our destiny.
The other soldier talked to me about his hometown,
    Bovalino. (22)
We talked about many other things
We traveled together until Taranto. (23)
After which, we went our separate ways.

We arrived in the city of Taranto
And our paths diverged.
I was preoccupied.
I boarded the train for Lecce,
Which was ready to depart.
We arrived in Brindisi. (24)
I saw some disturbing things.
Some soldiers were standing nearby.
They said, "Here you cannot act like you are an ordinary
    citizen.
You have to commit yourself to being a soldier."

---

(22) Bovalino, a town in the province of Reggio Calabria, is located 40 miles east of Reggio Calabria on the coast of the Ionian Sea.

(23) Taranto is the capital of the Province of Taranto. It is a coastal city in Apulia, Southern Italy on the Ionian Sea. Taranto was founded by the Spartans in about 700 B.C.E..

(24) Brindisi is the capital of the Province of Brindisi, a coastal city in Apulia, Southern Italy. It is on the Adriatic Sea, 45 miles east of Taranto.

Allora io mi dispiacea
Perche' a Brindisi non potea vedere
Noi comandati siamo missero a mea
E dobiamo fare il nostro dovere
Di sentinella siamo vicino a tea
E percio' tu non puoi trasire
Il treno venne; missero a mia
l'ora e' giunta e tu deve partire
Dopo un'ora il treno legermente
Finalmente arrivammo a Lecce
Sono arivato alla stazione
Ecco il paese dei mangiacane
Erano avanzate le nove
E delle grida non si poteva stare
Con disturbo e con confusione
Io ero morto di sete e con tanta fame
La cerano le nostre piantone
Venite vi volemo accompagnare
Dormo nella paglia come il Bambino
E quello era il mio destino

I was unhappy
Because I was not allowed to see Brindisi.
They told me, "You are under orders.
We have to do our duty.
We are sentries and we are watching you.
You cannot go into Brindisi."
Alas, the train was arriving; they said to me.
"The hour has arrived and you must leave."
After an hour's slow train ride,
We finally reached Lecce. (25)

I arrived at the station
This is a town of thieves and liars [mangiacane] (26)
It was after nine in the evening.
It was hard to put up with all the shouting,
Turmoil and confusion.
I was dying of thirst and very hungry.
The sentries said,
"Come with us, we will escort you."
I was to sleep in the hay like baby Jesus
And that was my destiny.

Io la notte non dormiva
Penzava la mia mala sfortuna
Come il cane a terra mi malediceva
Arivando in caserma a tarda ora
E a fare un'ora di camino
Con molto freddo e aria scura
Mi hanno dato un paglione e un cuscino
Puzzava come la sepoltura
Era una vita che si doveva fare
Le patimente le veniva assagiare
Aveva un letto duro come un molino
Penzava il paese dei porci
Dopo sei giorni vado alla misura
Un mi totera misero nei fantocci
Era molto alto di statura
Occominciava a vedere le pidocchi
La fanteria non ha mai paura
Mi portaro le robbe sporche
Erano piene di lordura
Come le Turche della Mezzaluna

The Tomb

After an hour's walk
In the cold and the dark,
We arrived at the barracks at a late hour.
I was condemned to sleep on the floor like a dog.
They gave me a straw mattress and a pillow.
The barracks had the stench of a tomb.
All night I laid awake.
I was thinking of my misfortune.
This was the life I had to endure.
I came to taste suffering.

My bed was as hard as a millstone.
For me Lecce was a town of pigs.
After six days, I went to be measured [for my uniform]
A soldier among puppets
I was of tall stature.
I began to see lice.
The infantry is never afraid.
They brought me dirty clothes.
They were full of filth
Like the Turks of the Half Moon. (27)

---

(25)...Lecce is 25 miles south of Brindisi and eight miles from the Adriatic coast (see footnote 20, p.37).

(26) "Mangiacane" appears to be an abbreviation of the Sicilian curse, "Ti putissiru mangiari li cane [May the dogs devour you]!" Plutarch identifies a temple dedicated to the god Adranus (Hadranos), who was the protector of Sicily, on the slope of Mount Etna. The temple was guarded by one thousand dogs, Cirneco dell'Etna, a breed indigenous to Sicily. The dogs greeted and guided faithful pilgrims. The dogs recognized and attacked thieves and perjurers without mercy. (Fiorentino, Paolo. *Sicily through Symbolism and Myth: Gates to Heaven and the Underworld.* Mineola, NY: Legus, 2006, pp. 37-38).

(27) The term Turche (Turks) would have carried with it disdain for a formidable and longtime enemy of Italy and Europe, the Ottoman Empire. (Continued)

Queste erano l'Italiane
Si vestiro come li zampaglione
Nella citta' si misero a passegiare
Parivano tutte come li cafoni
Con la divisa da militare
Mi scusate miei signore
Parevamo tutte maiale
Nei paesa dei lordume
Eramo e sporche come gli animale
Nel paese dei mangiacane
Ma io sempre penzando
Che a Squinzano doveva andare
La sera a Squinzano arivammo
Vestite come gli rufiane
La notte veniva avanzando
Che brutta vita e' il militare
A mio fratello andavo trovando
Non sapeva dove lo posso trovare
Disse il Comandante qui ce la disciplina
Tuo fratello lo vedi domane mattina

It was the Italians
Who dressed us like clowns.
We started strolling the streets of Lecce.
We all looked like dolts
Dressed in our military uniforms.
Please excuse me ladies and gentlemen,
But we looked like pigs,
In this pigsty of a town.
We were filthy, like animals,
In this town of thieves and liars [mangiacane].

I was preoccupied, thinking
That I had to go to Squinzano. (28)
That evening we arrived in Squinzano,
Dressed like ruffians.
It was almost nighttime.
What a bad life, to be in the Army.
I was looking for my brother and
I did not know where to find him.
The Commander said, "Here we have rules.
You will see your brother tomorrow morning."

---

(27)...For hundreds of years, the Ottoman Empire ruled the Muslim world and was involved in many wars with Christian Europe. In October 1571, a fleet composed of a European alliance defeated the fleet of the Ottoman Empire at the Battle of Lepanto, but the Ottoman Empire quickly recovered from this defeat. The mezzaluna (half moon in Italian) along with a star was a symbol of the Ottoman Empire and is seen on Turkey's current flag.

The precise origin of the mezzaluna symbol is unclear. There are many accounts. One story states that Philip II of Macedonia, in about 340 B.C.E., attacked the walls of Byzantium under the cover of darkness. His plan was thwarted by a sudden wind that blew the clouds away, allowing the previously hidden crescent moon to provide the light that allowed the sentinels of Byzantium to see the danger and sound the alarm. As a result, the Macedonian attack failed. In thanks, the citizens carved the crescent moon into many stone artifacts of the city. After the Ottoman Turks captured Constantinople in 1453, they saw the crescent moon symbol carved in stone structures of the city and adopted it as their own symbol. (Continued)

E sotto l'Arme troppo si sofriva
La sveglia si intese tutta squilando
Cera un freddo e un' aria fina
Sergente e caporale tutte gridando
Alzatevi che e' mattina
Le truzione tutte marciammo
Tutte a linea e a fila
Finalmente al posto arrivammo
Ci facevano a tutte stentare
Massimamente i caporale
Io ci disse al mio officiale
Un giorno ave e non ne posso ciune
Con mio fratello voleva stare
Non qui a fare le istruzione
La domanda dovete fare
e al caporale ce la done
Per via geartica deve passare
L'ave a leggere il maggiore
Era Sardegnolo l'officiale
Con mio fratello non mi ha voluto passare

In the Army, there is much suffering.
We heard the blare of the bugle calling reveille.
It was really cold and the air was frosty.
The Sergeant and Corporal came in yelling,
"Get up, it is morning.
We have to practice marching."
We marched all in a line, one after another
Finally we arrived at our destination.
They made us all stand at attention,
Especially the Corporals.

I said to my superior,
"A day has passed and I cannot wait any longer.
I want to be with my brother,
Not here taking part in basic training."
"You have to make a written request
And give it to your Corporal.
You have to go through official channels
The Major has to approve it."
The Officer was from Sardinia
He would not allow me to go to see my brother.

---

(27)...In addition to war, there were cultural exchanges and cooperation
between Europe and the Ottoman Empire. The interactions of Muslim,
Jewish and Christian scholars are legion. There were also many
military alliances between parts of the Ottoman world and Christian
powers in Europe.

(28) Squinzano is located in the Apulia region of southern Italy and is
10 miles north of Lecce.

Cera un Palermitano con un pugnale
Disse non voglio fare istruzione
Allora ordina l'officiale
Me lo portano in prigione
Non si voleva fare pigliare
Protestava che voleva stare fuori
Dicendo mi volete arestare
Vi faro' vedere carognone
Allora il tenente la spada sfoderando
Lo stesso fa il soldato gridando.
Allora l'ordine del infame
Che fanno la legge senza ragione
Lo accompagno' un Caporale
Dopo due giorni fu meso fuore
Il tenente lo vozze perdonare
Un'altra volta alle istruzione
Quello si metteva a guardare
Non obbediva piu'alle superiore
Il tenente ci disse sono Napolitano
Il soldato disse sono Palermitano.

A Soldier Objects

There was a soldier from Palermo (29) with a dagger.
He said, "I don't want to take part in basic training."
So the officer ordered,
"Take him to the lockup."
He did not want to be taken.
He was protesting that he wanted to remain free
Saying, "You want to arrest me.
I will show you, you low-lifes."
So the Lieutenant took his sword out of its sheath.
The soldier did the same thing while screaming.

Then following the orders of those disgraceful people,
Who make unreasonable laws,
A Corporal took him to the lockup.
After two days, they released him.
The Lieutenant wanted to pardon him
And return him to basic training.
But the soldier just stood there watching.
He no longer obeyed orders.
Finally the Lieutenant said, "I am from Naples." (30)
The soldier retorted, "I am from Palermo."

---

(29) Palermo was founded in 734 B.C.E. by Phoenicians and is the
capital of Sicily. Over the centuries Sicily has endured a series of
invaders. One of its interesting rulers was the Holy Roman Emperor
Frederick II (December 1272-June 1337). He was an erudite, energetic
genius who was nicknamed Stupor Mundi (Wonder of the World). He
spoke six languages: Latin, Sicilian, German, French, Greek and
Arabic. His poetry was highly praised. Frederick encouraged Italian
vernacular poetry. This "Sicilian School" of poetry influenced Dante
who considered Frederick II the father of Italian poetry. Nonetheless,
Dante put Frederick II in a fiery grave in the circle of heresy (Circle 6,
Canto 10, line 119).

(30) Naples was founded by Greek settlers in the second millennium
B.C.E. and is the third largest city in Italy. In 1137, Norman Roger II,
King of Sicily, conquered Naples. (Continued)

Tutte in caserma arivamo
Di struzione non ne voleva sentire
Lui si incazza con armata mano
A nessuno poteva piu' vedere
Adiventa come un vulcano
Con l'occhi rosse potete credere
Pareva che lo focaro
Certo lui pareva una tighe
Lui disse io guerra non ne faccio
Portatemi in pregione sono pazzo
Di quel giorno non lo potte piu' vedere
Al manicomio lo vozzero portare
Dopo 8 giorni mi portaro a me alle tire
Al Bersaglio vicino al mare
La marcia di corsa potete credere
Al Bersaglio mi devo sparare
Amice miei venite a sentire
Quanto e brutto il militare
Mi si alza presto la mattina
Col freddo e con l'acquazzina

We all went to the barracks
But that soldier continued not to obey orders.
Then, he became angry and took out his weapon.
He would not listen to reason.
He erupted like a volcano;
His eyes filled with rage.
He looked like he was on fire.
He seemed like a ferocious tiger.
He said, "I am not going to war.
Take me to prison, I am crazy."

They took him to the insane asylum
From that day on, I never saw him again.
After eight days, they took us for target practice
At a shooting range near the sea.
You can believe me, we marched double-time.
To get to the shooting range where we took target practice.
My friends come and listen,
It is horrible to be in the Army.
We had to get up very early
Every morning to engage in basic training
In the cold and the rain.

---

(30)...His grandson Frederick II (Stupor Mundi) founded the first state university in the world in Naples. It included a medical school that developed standards for the practice of medicine and required that doctors be licensed in order to practice. Of note, Antonio Ciccone (February 6, 1808-May 2, 1891), a distant relative, was a Professor of Political Economy at the University of Naples. He was also a Doctor of Medicine (Annals of the American Academy of Political and Social Science IV: 111-112, 1894).

Di fare istruzione ogni mattina
Venivamo a caserma ha riposare
Alle 10 ci mettevamo a fila
Per quattro dovevamo marciare
Era male di ogni sera
E della stanchezza non poteva stare
Il soldato era una rovina
A dormire a terra come il cane
Stanco poi mi mettevoa a dormire
Doveva sempre polizare il fucile
Io tante cose non le poteva sofrire
Dormivo a lumido dentro una cantina
Per caserma era uno scentino
Ogni notte cera l'aria fina
Questo e certo e ve lo posso dire
Ogni mattina cera la sveglia
Chi considera puo' credere
A me mi pariva una maciavella
Era una vita di patimente
60 giorni ho fatto di permanente

Basic Training Continues

We returned to the barracks to rest.
At ten a.m., we had to line up
Four abreast and we had to march.
Every night I was exhausted.
I could not shed the fatigue.
The life of a soldier was destructive to me.
I had to sleep on the ground like a dog.
At times, I was so tired I would fall asleep while cleaning
    my rifle.

There were many things I could not bear.
Since the barrack was a cellar,
It was like sleeping in a damp crypt,
I can tell you this for certain,
Every night the air was biting cold.
Each morning there was reveille.
Those of you paying attention can believe that
It was like I was being crushed by a massive millstone,
A life of suffering
That lasted for sixty straight days.

Erano ore e pure momente
E venuta la partenza per partire
Una mattina la sveglia si sente
Alzatevi non si puo' dormire
Dovete stare tutti allegramente
Siamo alle 13 aprile
Questa e' sonata malamente
Dovemo ora tutte partire
Venerdi era giorno disgraziato
Con mio fratello io partiva a lato
Partimo con un certo Lionello
Di Sinopoli era il creatore
Allora partimo con molto risveglio
Partimo in marcia per la stazione
Era un giorno caldo e bello
Ma io era in tribolazione
Il treno era venuto presto
I soldate erano con male amore
Tutte le borghese si misero a gridare
Le bandiere vennero a sventolare.

Friday, April 13, 1917

We counted the hours and even the minutes.
Then one morning we heard reveille
And the order, "Get up. You can no longer sleep.
You should all be glad."
The hour for our departure had arrived.
At this point, it was April 13th
This was terrible news.
Now we all had to leave
This Friday was my unlucky day
With my brother at my side, I left [Squinzano].

We left with a certain Lionello,
From Sinopoli, (31) who was a good soul.
We resigned ourselves to our fate.
We marched to the station in formation.
It was a warm, beautiful day
But I was very troubled.
The train arrived early.
The soldiers were in a bad mood.
All of the people in the town began cheering
And waving Italian flags.

---

(31) Sinopoli is a municipality that is one mile east of Sant'Eufemia
d'Aspromonte. In 1911, it had a population of 4,000 inhabitants.

Allora il treno ci venne a salutare
Partiva io col mio compagno
Certi soldate si misero a cantare
Io e l'amico penzavamo tanto
Che in guerra dovevamo andare
Ma io sempre penzando
Lasciava la citta' vicino al mare
Penzava il passato mormorando
Il destino fu e la mia mala sfortuna
E' partito il treno verso l'una
Passammo tutta la pianura
Il treno caminava vicino al mare
Penzava la mia terra pura
Perche' in America non vozze stare
Era pallida la mia persona
Che al fronte dovevo andare
Faceva un bel tempo adirittura
Finalmente arrivammo a Bari
Tutto il popolo si mise a trionfare
Passano le soldate italiane

The train was there to greet us.
I left with my friend.
Some soldiers began to sing.
My friend and I were preoccupied,
We were compelled to go to war.
That is all I could think about.
As we left the city by the sea [Squinzano],
I was thinking about the past and quietly said to myself,
"It is my destiny and my misfortune."
The train left at about one o'clock.

As we crossed the entire plain,
The train traveled along the shore.
While thinking of my dear country,
I thought to myself, "Why didn't I stay in America?"
I was ashen
Thinking about having to go to the front.
The weather was good and
Finally the train arrived in Bari. (32)
The people began jubilantly cheering us,
"The Italian soldiers are passing through."

---

(32) Bari, the capital city of the Province of Bari, is located on the
Adriatic Sea about 85 miles north of Squinzano.

Si venne il treno a distaccare
Con la furia del vento partiva
Il treno fugiva per solicitare
Gli Abruzze poco io le distinguiva
Quando a Rimini ci vennommo a fermare
Giorno 15 era la sera
Mi venne subito a dolorare
Disse io fu una mala spina
Disse a Lionello io ho fame
Andiamo subito a mangiare
Dopo finito da pranzare
Andiamo di corsa per la Stazione
Il treno se ne voluto andare
Con spavento non lo vittimo ciune
Partiva con 600 militari
Tra soldate e caporal maggiore
Io mi mise col compagno a passeggiare
Nella citta' di Rimini era il suo nome
I carabinieri erano di piantone
Mi dissero dateci le vostre cognome

Sunday, April 15, 1917

Then the train departed
Traveling fast as a furious wind.
The train raced ahead.
After a while, I could make out Abruzzi (33)
When we arrived in Rimini (34) we stopped.
It was the evening of the 15th
I was filled with anguish.
It was dread that overcame me.
I told Lionello, "I'm hungry.
Let's go eat now."

After we finished eating,
We ran back to the station.
The train was leaving and
We were terrified as we watched it disappear.
It left with six hundred military men
Comprised of soldiers and non-commissioned officers.
Along with my companion, I began walking in the city,
Rimini was its name,
The police were patrolling
And they asked for our names.

---

(33) Abruzzi is a mountainous region of central Italy on the Adriatic
Sea. Pescara, a coastal city in the Abruzzi region, is approximately 190
miles north of Bari.

(34) Rimini is a city in the Emilia-Romagna region of Italy. On the
coast of the Adriatic Sea, it is approximately 160 miles north of
Pescara.

Ci disse mi chiamo Giuseppe Ciccone
Sono Calabrese disse alle carabiniere
Non credete che sono un disertore
Di oggi innanze fate il vostro dovere
Partite subito al campo dell'onore
La Patria dovete difendere
Che e' la nostra bandiera il tre colore
Noi andiamo tutte a morire
Disse io con parole incazzate
E voi altri assassini siete imboscati
Pigliamo noi il treno per partire
Noi andavamo al tiro del cannone
Tutta l'alta Italia vozze preseguire
Molte imboscate e molte ladrone
Il basso popolo andava a morire
Per causa di quei vile dei signore
La guerra ora la veniva a vedere
Per causa di Cecco Peppe e Guglielmone
Dello spavento mi tremavano lossa
A Padova cera la croci Rossa

I replied, "My name is Giuseppe [Joseph] Ciccone."
I went on, "I am Calabrese [I am from Calabria],
Do not think that I am a deserter."
He said, "From this day forward, do your duty.
Leave immediately for the field of honor.
You have to defend our country.
It is our flag, the tricolor flag."
I responded in rageful words,
"We are going to die,
While you cowards are shirking military service."

We took the train and departed.
We were going into the line of fire.
While rich Italians wanted to continue the war
Those shirkers and frauds were avoiding military service,
The lower class Italians were going to die.
I was getting ready to face war
Because of Frankie-Joey and Willie,
I was overcome by fear and was trembling.
In Padua there was a unit of the Red Cross.

Il treno si ferma con una scossa
Chi disse al compagno ferma ccane
Io mi apresento alla croce Rossa
Ci disse ave un giorno che ho fame
Le dame mi fecero una mossa
Pigliaro 4 uova e un pane
Ci disse voi altre la sapete grossa
Ci trattate molto male
La marsala la tenete per le imboscate
Me ne donano un bicchiere arabiati
Allora io parto per le strade
Arivo dove era il mio compagno
Lionello si voleva chiamare
Di Sinopoli mancava di tanto
Il treno si mise subito a marciare
Alle nostre confine insomma arivammo
A Cervegnano vennomo arivare
Nelle terre austriece calammo
A l'osteria andammo a mangiare

When the train came to a jolting stop in Padua, (35)
I said to my companion [Lionello], "Wait here."
I went to the Red Cross
And told them that I had not eaten all day and I was
　　hungry.
The Red Cross ladies acknowledged me.
They gave me four eggs and a loaf of bread.
I said, "All of you live high on the hog.
You treat us miserably.
You keep the marsala (36) for the cowards who hide from
　　military service."
They were annoyed but gave me a glass of marsala.

I left and walked back.
I arrived to where my friend was waiting,
Lionello was his name;
He had been away from Sinopoli for a long time.
Shortly after I got back, the train left.
We arrived near the Italian-Austrian border.
We arrived in Cervignano (37)
In the ill-fated Austrian territory.
Now we Italians were there.
We went to the tavern to eat.

-----

(35) Traveling via Bologna, Padua is about 140 miles north of Rimini.
Padua is in the Veneto about 25 miles west of Venice.

(36) Marsala wine is produced in the area around Marsala, Sicily using
the Grillo, Inzolia and Catarratto white grapes. Most wines have 12.5%
to 14.5% alcohol content. Marsala is a fortified wine that is an aperitif
and is often used in cooking. It is made by adding brandy at the
appropriate time during fermentation, wihich kills the yeast and ends
the fermentation process. Marsala often contains 17 to 18% alcohol.

(37) Cervignano del Friuli is a town in the province of Udine located
about 70 miles northeast of Venice and 30 miles east of Trieste.
Cervignano is about 11 miles from the Adriatic. It is about 95 miles
northeast of Padua.

Alle 10 ve lo voglio dire
Partimo per le parte di Sagrade
Eravamo nelle vecchie confine
Prima era austrieco il locale
Io senza zaino e senza fucile
Della paura non potevo stare
A Sagrado vozzemo scendire
E per gradisca ci misomo a camminare
La cera la carneficina
Era bombardato pure Trausina
Come e venuta la mattina
Io caminava col mio compagno
Nemmeno aveva la mia mantellina
Gli ufficiali per sdrata incontrammo
Si incazzano con male ira
Dove eravo dissero mormorando
Perdemmo il treno ieri sera
Ora dovete andare al comando
Voi altri siete ora disertore
Vi attocca presto la prigione

Arrival at Sagrado/48th Regiment, 3rd Company

It was ten o'clock when
We left to go to Sagrado. (38)
We were within the old borders,
Before it was Austrian territory.
I was without a backpack and without a rifle.
I was scared to death.
We got off the train at Sagrado
And made our way to Gradisca (39)
It was like a slaughterhouse.
Sdraussina (40) had also been bombarded.

As dawn arrived,
I was walking with my friend.
I did not even have a cape.
While walking, we came across officers.
They were angry and full of rage
They asked, "Where have you been?"
I mumbled, "We missed the train last night."
"Now you have to go to headquarters
Both of you are deserters and
You should go right to prison."

---

(38) Sagrado is 22 miles northwest of Trieste, six miles east of Cervignano del Friuli, and is near Monte San Michele. Fierce fighting between Italian and Austro-Hungarian troops occurred on Monte San Michele during World War I.

(39) Gradisca d'Isonzo is located three miles north of Sagrado and is on the right bank of the Isonzo River. In 1914, at the outbreak of WWI, the population of Gradisca as well as Gorizia, Trieste and Trento were living in Austrian territory. The Italians living there fought under the Austria-Hungarian banner. Gradisca became part of Italy in 1921.

(40) Sdraussina is a town near Sagrado. It is now called Poggio Terza Armata.

Andammo subito al maggiore
E lui non ne fece niente
Io vi perdono per 24 ore
Vi asegno al 48 reggimente
Ora disse si sente il cannone
Coraggio soldate con argomente
Qui si campa ho si muore
Dobbiamo essere prudente
Morimo sul campo del onore
E io sono del primo battagione
Ognuno deve fare il suo dovere
Sono passato alla 3° Compagnia
Con fedelta' dovete servire
Mi portano subito in foreria
A me mi vennero le bile
Il mio compagno non lo vedea
Unito al mio compagno voglio ghire
Fate silenzio mi dissero a mia
Di ora innanze fate il vostro dovere
Se no vi incatenamo coli carabiniere

We went right to the Major
And the Major chose not to punish us.
"I will pardon you for being twenty-four hours late.
I am assigning you to the 48th Regiment.
Then he said, "You can hear the cannons."
He exhorted us, "Have courage soldiers.
We have to be careful.
On this field we will live or die.
If we die, it will be on the field of honor."
I was a part of the First Battalion,

And assigned to the Third Company.
Everyone must do his duty
And we have to serve with loyalty.
They quickly brought me to the company office.
I became angry and consumed with rage because
I could not find my friend Lionello.
"I want to go and be assigned with my friend."
"Be quiet," they told me.
"From now on follow orders.
If not, we will have the MPs incarcerate you."

Allora io mi incazzo come una tighe
Infami siete e carognone
Io so fare il mio dovere
Ma io voglio essere al quel battaglione
Dissero con lui non puoi sire
Deve stare qui a questo battaglione
Siete una razza di gente vile
Facete la legge alle vostre mode
Nemmeno puoi stare con tuo fratello
Conortete ora che e' meglio
Allora al mio compagno Lionello
Al battaglione marciante andava
Dopo due giorni di quello successo
A linea io andava
Fuoco di artiglieria come il castello
Di ogni parte si infuriava
Faceva la carcara dell'inferno
Dove Pluto la attizzava
Lavorava e faceva il mio dovere
Sparavano tutte le calabri l'artigliere

I became an enraged beast.
"You despicable cowards,
I know how to do my duty.
But I want to go to the other battalion."
They replied, "You cannot be with your friend.
You have to stay with this battalion."
I responded, "You are a race of vile people.
You make the laws as you please."
They said, "You cannot even be with your brother.
Understand, it is better this way."

The Frontline– 15 Days

So my friend Lionello
Marched to the other battalion.
Two days after the confrontation with the Major,
I went to the front line.
The artillery fire lit up the sky
This furious bombardment came from everywhere. (41)
It was like the depths of hell
Where Pluto stokes the fires. (42)
I was working and doing my duty.
The artillerymen were all Calabrese.

---

(41) A number of weapons were invented or first used in World War I, creating what has been called mechanized slaughter. They include the airplane, tanks, flame throwers, tracer bullets, torpedoes, depth charges, the Zeppelin and poison gas. Barbed wire and steel helmets were also first used in WWI.

(42) Pluto is one of the six children of Cronus and Rhea and the brother of Zeus and Poseidon. Pluto ruled the underworld. Pluto and Plutus (the god of wealth) are closely associated. As far back as the Greeks and Romans, Pluto "was considered to be the god of riches as well as the ruler of the underworld." (Singleton, C.S. *Inferno 2. Commentary,* 1970, pp. 109-110.)

Torquato Tasso portrayed Pluto as a satanic figure in *Jerusalem Delivered.* In Canto VII of Dante's *Inferno,* Virgil and Dante encounter Pluto. (Continued)

Stavamo a lavorare tutte alegre
Sentivamo l'ordine del officiale
Parola dietro fronte venne a dire
A l'Austriece lavemo a scannare
Le mitragliatrice si vennero a sentire
Di quelle maledette e infame
Di ogni parte sparavano con i fucile
L'inferno cera del areoprane
Come la tempesta con le tuone
E ci pigliavano a colpi di cannone
Dopo 15 giorni di dolori
Venne il nostro cambiamento
Andiamo a riposo disse il magiore
Uscimo un poco di questo inferno
Dietro non siamo a tiro di cannone
Sento il cambio ed era contento
Sento il carso e mi lamento
E' la terra dei diavolone
Che sono sempre nel fuoco eterno
La fucina di Pluto era a Monfalcone

We were working as one.
We had our orders from the Officer.
Word came from behind the front that
We must slaughter the Austrians.
We heard machine gun fire
From those damned, infamous people.
From all around us they were also shooting at us with rifles.
Their airplanes were creating their own hell
And they were hitting us with cannon fire.
It was like a tempest punctuated by thunder.

Relief– May 3, 1917

After 15 days of this suffering
Our relief arrived [the 20th Regiment].
"We are going to rest," said the Major.
"Let's get out of this hell for a while.
In the rear, we will be out of range of the cannon fire."
I heard that we were relieved and I was happy.
I heard the sounds on the Carso (43) and I was anguished.
This is the land of Satan.
Here, we are always in the eternal fire.
Pluto's forge was at Monfalcone. (44)

---

(42)...Pluto is guarding the fourth circle of hell and marvels that a
living man is walking through Hell. He is worried that he may be in
danger and calls for Satan's help:

> "Pape Satan, pape Satan aleppe!"
> So Plutus, with his grating voice, began.
> The gentle sage, aware of everything
> said reassuringly, "Don't let your fear
> defeat you; for whatever power he has,
> he cannot stop our climbing down this crag."
> Then he turned back to Plutus' swollen face
> and said to him: "Be quiet, cursed wolf!
> Let your vindictiveness feed on yourself."

(Mandelbaum, A. *Inferno*. Berkeley, California: University of
California Press, 1980, p. 54.) (Continued)

A mezza notte venne il 20°
Reggimento con il suo onore
Noi tutte di corsa fugendo
Fino che arrivammo a vallone
Io era molto contento
Andava a riposo non si sapeva a dove
Caminavamo a passo svelto
Spaventate tutte del terrore
Arrivammo alle 5 la mattina
Nelle baracche a Traisina
Io mi mise subito a dormire
Stanco ero di quello caminare
Sento un spavento che non si puo' dire
Cerano in aria 10 areopraine
Io allora mi mise a fugire
Per monte S. Michele a scappare
Parole di ferma non vozze sentire
Era vita di potermi salvare
Fuggio senza il fucile
E mi rifugio sotto ale pine

At midnight the 20th Regiment, (45)
With its distinguished reputation, arrived to relieve us.
We all ran from the Carso
Until we reached the Vallone. (46)
I was very happy.
I was going to get some rest but I did not know where.
We were walking at a brisk pace.
We were all terrorized.
At five in the morning, we arrived
At the barracks at Sdraussina.

I was so tired from that five-hour walk
That I quickly fell asleep.
I awoke with a fear beyond words.
There were ten enemy airplanes overhead.
I tried to escape
And began running toward Monte San Michele (47)
I did not want to hear the order to stop.
I was trying to save my life.
I ran without my rifle
And took refuge in a pine forest.

---

(42)...Ciardi, commenting about the opening of Canto VII, wrote,
"Plutus menaces the Poets, but once more Virgil shows himself more
powerful than the rages of Hell's monsters." (Cardi, J. *The Divine
Comedy*, 1970, p. 34). The meaning of the line, "Pape Satan, pape
Satan aleppe!" is not entirely clear. "Pape" may reflect astonishment
and "aleppe" may express pain. Singleton quotes Boccaccio's
Commento: "Pluto marvels, then, for this is something never seen
hitherto: That a living man should be walking through Hell. Fearing
that this may redound to his harm, he invokes the aid of his superior."
(Singleton, C.S. *Inferno 2. Commentary*. 1970, pp. 108-109).

(43) The Carso (also known as the Karst Plateau) is a limestone
plateau, a land of rock that steeply descends into the Adriatic Sea. It is
known for its caves, difficult terrain, strong Bora winds and cold
temperatures. "The Carso is probably the strongest natural fortress in
the world. Anything in the shape of defensive works which Nature had
overlooked, the Austrians provided." E. Alexander Powell, American
Journalist, 1916. Sagrado, Sdraussina, Monfalcone and Trieste are
entirely or partially located in the Carso.

I nemici volevano bombardare
Sferra la nostra artiglieria
L'Austriece scapparo con le areoprane
Noi altre eramo dietro una trincea
Due si vozzero bruciare
Questo e' il valore dell'artiglieria
Sempre e' sangue dei Italiane
A l'austria la distrugge la fanteria
Siamo Italiani di volere
Scacciamo l'austria sotto le piede
Dopo di tanto non successe piu' niente
Andiamo tutte alle estruzione
Dopo 10 giorni una notizia si sente
Ci calavano a tutte le pantalone
Il Maggiore disse andiamo all'accampamento
In ordine ci mise con dolore
Alle figlio era la mia mente
Giovanotti disse il maggiore
State tutte allegramenti
Chi muore per la padria non e' niente

The enemy was bombing us.
Our aircraft artillery answered.
The Austrian planes retreated.
All of us were in a trench.
Two Austrian planes went down in flames.
This is the value of the artillery.
Courageous Italian blood flows through our veins.
Austria will be destroyed by our infantry.
We Italians have a strong will.
We will crush the Austrians under our feet.

After the planes left, things went quiet.
We went for military training.
After ten days, we received notice.
We were all shaking in our boots.
The Major said, "We are going to the encampment."
I fell into formation in anguish,
My thoughts went to my son.
"Young men," said the Major,
"Be of good spirit.
Dying for your country is an honor.

---

(44) Monfalcone is six miles south of Gradisca d'Isonzo and is located
on the Gulf of Trieste. It sits between the Carso and the Adriatic Sea.
Monfalcone was captured by Italy during World War I. Austria
recaptured it after the battle of Caporetto (October 24 to November 12,
1917). After World War I, it returned to Italy.

(45) The 20th Regiment was part of the Brescia Brigade.

(46) Vallone is the name of a large valley that runs north-south in the
Carso Plain.

(47) Monte San Michele is six miles north of Monfalcone and two
miles north of Doberdò del Lago.

Dobbiamo andare al campo del onore
Io sono pure un Calabrese
La ho si campa ho si muore
S. Biase e il mio paese
Barbetta Egilio e' il mio nome
Manco di casa di due anni e piu' mese
Coraggio soldate disse con furore
Viva li soldati Calabrese
Sono tutte al mio Battaglione
L'avete calabrese il vostro maggiore
C'erano Siciliane e pure Barese
A tutte bene lui le volia
Arivando al campo ci donno le camicie
Che la sera dovemo andare in trincea
L'avanzata si intese
E tutto il Carso ardea
Il Colonnello era di Tropea
Ce fece la propraganda con dolce parole
Questa e' l'ultima azione

We must go to the field of honor.
There we will live or die."
The Major went on, "I am also Calabrese.
S. Biase is my hometown.
My name is Egilio Barbetta
I have been away for more than two years."
With fervor the Major said, "Be courageous.
I salute the Calabrese soldiers
In my Battalion
Your Major is also Calabrese."

There were soldiers from Sicily and from Bari.
The Major was good to all of us.
Arriving at the camp, they gave us shirts
At night, we had to go into the trenches.
The fighting intensified.
The Carso was ablaze.
We were soldiers from all over Italy
The Colonel was from Tropea. (48)
With sweet words, he provided us with propaganda,
"This is the last battle."

---

(48) Tropea is a town in Calabria on the gulf of Sant'Eufemia,
approximately 60 miles north of Sant'Eufemia d'Aspromonte.

Il 12 di maggio un'altra volta saliva
Al Carso cera il bombardamento
Arrivammo a Vallone alle 11 di sera
E ci fermammo tutto il Reggimento
Il carantotto era e della terza compagnia
La mattina ho veduto a mio fratello
La notte ci aspettava in trincea
Cera il purgatorio e pure l'inferno
Subito a mio fratello vozze abbraciare
Che contentezza io potte trovare
Questo ci succede a tutte pari
La guerra era la mia rovina
La se ne parlava di bobardare
4 giorni mattina e sera
Ci disse a mio fratello siamo tutte eguale
Che cosi' a voluto la mala spina
E ci dovemo tutte conortare
Che cosi' ha voluto la sorte assassina
A mezza notte sul Faite cera come le tighe
30 persone vennero a morire

The Tenth Battle of the Isonzo

The 12th of May [1917] arrived (49) and
The Carso was being bombarded.
We arrived at the Vallone at eleven p.m.
And the entire regiment came to a halt,
The 48th Regiment. I was part of the 3rd company.
The next morning, I saw my brother.
I immediately wanted to embrace him.
What a joy to have found him.
We expected to spend the night in the trenches.
It was purgatory and even hell.

Everyone came to understand
That the war was our total ruination.
There all we could talk about was the bombardment
That went on for four days from morning to night.
I told my brother, "We are all equal.
This is what fate has willed.
We all have to resign ourselves
That this is the will of murderous destiny."
At midnight on the Faite, (50) I was like a wild animal.
30 people died.

---

(49) On Saturday, May 12, 1917, the Italian Artillery opened fire along
the front and the 10th Battle of the Isonzo began.

"The first definite signs of an impending Italian drive on the Julian
front [the northeastern Italian Alps] appeared on May 12, 1917. Along
the whole front between Tolmino and the sea the Italians were active
with artillery and mine throwers. The fire lasted through the entire
night. It caused explosions and fires in the Austrian lines and was
continued with unabated vigor in spite of prompt response from the
Austrian guns during May 13, 1917." (*The Story of the Great War*, Vol.
6, History of the European War from Official Sources. Kindle edition.
New York: P.F. Collier & Son, 1916, p. 461).

"The initial bombardment, when it was started on 12 May, was more
intense than anything the Austrians had seen before... Zero hour
followed at 12:00... (Continued)

Queste sono le nostre destine
Andava caricato come le bestiame
Stavo a traisina salvo di morire
E la di ogni parte venemmo a bobardare
Portava io bombe a mano e il fucile
Il Capitano si chiamava Dispone
Calabrese era e molto civile
Si conosceva al parlare
Trovatevi un recovero disse con energia
Io mi metto dentro un buco di galeria
Poi mi disse a mia
La vita a questo posto ve la potete sconzare
La migliore era la via
Io tremavo come tutte pare
Cera uno spirante pure con mia
Ci disse io qui non ti vene a incazzare
Vigliacco qui non tiene energia
Fatte forte con la rivoltella alle mane
A riposo sempre comandando
Alle 10 venne l'ordine del Comando

This is our destiny.
I had been safe in Sdraussina but
Here they bombarded us from every side.
I was loaded down like a beast of burden.
I carried hand grenades and a rifle.
The Captain's name was Dispone.
He was from Calabria and was very civil.
That was evident by the way he spoke.
He emphatically ordered us to take cover.
I put myself in the entrance of a tunnel

Then the Captain said to me,
"In this tunnel you may be able to save your life."
This was the best way to survive.
I was trembling like everyone else.
There was an Officer Cadet near me.
I said to him, "Doesn't this make you angry?
Coward, don't give up.
Get strong with your revolver in your hand."
We were resting and waiting for orders.
At ten o'clock, the Command's orders arrived.

---

(49)...On the central Carso, at the fortified line beyond the Vallone...
Halfway through the second day, the Third Army's losses stood at
25,000 men." (Thompson, Mark. *The White War: Life and Death on
the Italian Front 1915-1919.* New York: Basic Books, 2008, pp. 251-
253.)

On May 14 1917, two days after the initial bombardment had
commenced, the Italian infantry attacked.

(50) The Dosso Faiti is a mountain that stands about 1400 feet high
and is eight miles northeast of Monfalcone. This mountain is an area
that is now part of Slovenia and it is called Fajtji Hrib.

Dovevamo andare tutte all'asalto
Come le pecore senza padrone
Era un monte troppo alto
La linea di fuoco per ogni dove
Il Dosso Faite era il 14 maggio
L'ofenziva si faceva fino a Monfalcone
Alla linea nemica arivammo
Delle Austrieche di quelle infamone
E a tutte ci massagraro
Di ogni parte non cera riparo
Allora disse il nostro capitano
Tornate indietro con energia
In aria cera l'areoprano
Nascondetevi tutte nella trincea
La morte cera senza riparo
Di ogni parte si combattia
Di quanto e tenace l'Italiano
Le morte io li consava nella trincea
Io pregava tanto a S. Giuseppe
Mi mi libera di quelle tormente

We all had to go on the attack
Like sheep without a shepherd.
The mountain was very high.
We were being fired upon from every direction.
We were on the Dosso Faite and it was May 14th [1917]
The offensive line ran to Monfalcone.
We arrived at the enemy line
Of those infamous Austrians.
They were slaughtering us.
There was no place to take cover.

So our Captain ordered
Us to retreat quickly.
There were enemy planes overhead.
"Take cover in the trenches."
There was no shelter from death.
The fighting was everywhere.
The Italian soldiers were tough and tenacious.
I placed the dead in the trench
I was praying hard to St. Joseph
To free me from this torture.

Io ero come un cane arabiato
Con me c'era un caporal maggiore
Di Messina Gallo veniva chiamato
State attento soldato Ciccone
Io ci disse molto sidiato
Il ricalzo dietro tutto muore
Ci disse io come un lampato
Ho paura dentrolei pantalone
Di qui dobbiamo tutte le due fugire
Il tenente ci punta col fucile
Rispondo io Signor tenente
Ti prego mi butta il fucile
Io la vita comora non la penzo niente
Salvate se non vuoi morire
Qui ce l'inferno tutto ardente
La parola mia vozze obbidire
Ci penso io disse insolente
Quando andiamo a riposo ti metto a dovere
Le nemice lo vozzero mitragliare
Lui e morto con 17 pallottole all'ospedale

I was like a mad dog.
There was a Corporal Major with me
Named Gallo who was from Messina. He said,
"Be alert, Soldier Ciccone."
I told him with foreboding,
"The advancing reinforcements are all going to die."
Then I told him, like one lit up by lightening,
"I am scared to death.
We all have to get out of here."

The Lieutenant pointed his rifle at me.
I responded, "Lieutenant, with all due respect,
I beg you to put down your rifle.
At this moment, I am not thinking about my life.
Save yourself, if you do not want to die.
Here the fires of hell are ablaze."
The Lieutenant demanded, "You have to obey my orders."
I said to him insolently, "I'll think about it."
He replied, "When we get back, I will bring you up on
        charges."
The enemy fired at him with a machine gun.
He died in the hospital with seventeen bullets in him.

Io fuggio col caporal maggiore
E mi infilo dentro un caminamento
Perse il mio compagnone
Di cognome Gallo era scontento
Mi ariva un colpo di cannone
Allora io mi sgomento
Aresto alla trappola come un volpone
Faceva gride e pure lamento
Tutte credete miei care Signore
Che guai ho visto ho che terrore
Allora io tutto soffocato
Mi mise subito a gridare
Sotto le pietre arrestai sotterrato
Che mi aveva arivato un colpo di cannone
Compagne aiuto in questo misero stato
Ciccone mi vengo a chiamare
Allora corrono tutte a lato
Il nostro amico dissero le Siciliane
E senza dire una sola parola
Tempo 5 minuti fui stato fuori

Buried Alive

I fled with the Corporal Major [Gallo]
And climbed into a communication trench.
I was unhappy because
I lost my friend, Gallo.
Suddenly, I was hit by artillery fire.
I was panic-stricken.
Like a fox caught in a trap,
I was screaming and howling.
You can believe me, my dear men and women
What trouble and terrors were visited on me.

Then I began suffocating.
An artillery shell had hit near me
And I was buried under the rocks
I immediately started screaming.
"Friends, help me get out of this tomb.
My name is Ciccone."
Soldiers came running from all directions.
The Sicilians said, "He is our friend."
Without saying another word,
In five minutes, I was set free.

Signore miei venite a sentire
E tutte ascoltante i miei tormente
Il Tenente mi vozze dire
Sei tu ferito leggermente
E io subito ci vozze dire
Una gamba ho dolente
Dietro tu deve fugire
Disse quello amiatamente
Scappo come il serpe verso il Dottore
A centinaia erano le colpe di cannone
Ma io ancora non aveva niente
Di la vedevo un campanile
Il mare vicino a Trieste
8 cmi vicino a quelle terre
Questo e lo certe e ve lo posso garantire
E io vado al dottore ci disse solamente
Una gamba mi sento dolire
Questa mi disse non e niente
Allora mi disse il dottore
Vai dietro che qui si muore

My friends come and hear me,
And everyone listen to my torments.
The Lieutenant said,
"Your wounds are minor."
And I quickly replied,
"My leg hurts me."
He said forcefully,
"You have to withdraw quickly."
Crawling like a snake, I hurried toward the doctor.
Hundreds of artillery shells rained down on us.

Seeking Medical Attention

At this point, I still had not received any treatment.
From where I was, I could see a bell tower
And the sea near Trieste, (51)
That was eight kilometers [approximately five miles] away.
This is certain and I guarantee you,
I went to see the doctor and only said,
"My leg hurts."
The doctor told me that it was nothing
But then he said,
"Go to the rear because here we die."

---

(51) Trieste is an Italian seaport in the northeastern part of the Adriatic.
It was an Illyrian settlement in the second millennium B.C.E.. It came
under Austrian rule in 1382 and was the fourth largest city in the
Austrian-Hungarian Empire. Trieste was annexed by Italy in 1920 in
accordance with the treaty of Rapallo between the kingdom of Italy and
the Kingdom of the Serbs, Croats and Slovenes.

Scappo dietro amiatamente
Mi piglio di ferro un bastone
Il rincalzo era morto di quelli agente
Di tante colpa dei cannone
Vive quattro ho visto solamente
Io ho visto un deposito di munizione
Che era bruciato intotalmente
E valeva il costo di un milione
Caminava nel fuoco ardente
Vedo mule morte e pure conducente
Eravamo nelle fuoche ardente
La mia persona era spaventata
Molte ferite gravemente
Una Compagnia era sotterata
Allora io scrisciava come un serpe
Di Corizia al mare cera l'avanzata
Arivo dopo tante patimente
Con una gamba adolorata
Arrivo alla dollina delle tre taverne
E la mi feriro moltamente

I left the area quickly to get to the rear,
I grabbed a metal rod and used it as a walking stick.
The reinforcements had been killed
By the onslaught of artillery fire.
I saw only four of them alive.
I saw a deposit of munitions
That had exploded and was totally destroyed.
The value of the munitions was a million lire
I was walking in a scorching fire.
I saw dead mules and dead mule drivers

We were in this blazing fire.
My whole being was frightened.
Many were gravely injured.
A complete Company was buried under rubble
I was on the ground slithering like a snake.
The battle was raging from Gorizia (52) to the sea
I arrived after much suffering
With one leg in excruciating pain.
I arrived at the sink hole with three caves
And there I was injured more seriously.

_____

(52) Gorizia is about 13 miles north of Monfalcone.

Li credeva che sono salvate
Tempo un minuto fuo ferito
Di una scheggia di granate
Cascai a terra tramortito
Vennero le portaferite e mi pigliaro
E dentro la galleria mi portaro
La aveva un paesano
Mi disse Ciccone sei ferito
Monterosso era ed era bravo
E mi portano subito al Capitano
Dopo che bene mi medicava
Mi disse vai subito all'ospedale
Aiuto voglio io chiamava
Lui disse qui non puoi stare
Signor Capitano io bramava
Io non posso camminare
Mi devono portare entro una bara
Che sono ferito che non posso campare
Di me nessuno aveva compassione
Era a terra alla perdizione

Illusion of Safety

There I thought I was safe but
Within a minute I was wounded
By a shell fragment.
I fell to the ground unconscious.
The stretcher bearers came and took me
And they brought me inside a tunnel.
There I found someone from Calabria.
He said to me, "Ciccone, you are wounded."
His name was Monterosso and he was a good man.
He quickly took me to the Captain.

After they gave me first aid,
The Captain said to me, "Get to the hospital immediately."
"I want help," I implored.
He said, "You cannot stay here."
"Captain, Sir," I pleaded,
"I cannot walk.
They will have to carry me out in a coffin.
I am wounded and in more pain than I can bear."
No one had compassion for me.
I was on the ground in the middle of hell.

La dentro cera un soldato Siciliano
Io ci disse per piacere
Di qui l'Ospedale e lontano
Degli occhi miei io non ci vedo
Vedo scuro e cose strano
La galeria io non la vedo
Allora venne il capitano
Disse ho vai allo ospedale ho ti ucido
La rivoltella aveva alla mano
Vai via ho ti sparo
Io ci disse sono Italiano
Non austriaco come tu crede
E sono del sangue umano
E mi avanto te lo voglio dire
E bada bene Signor Capitano
Sono ferito e nessuno mi vede
Le miei parente sono lontano
Tengo un fratello qui vicino
Sto a terra 24 ore
Morto di sete e con gran dolore

In the tunnel, there was a Sicilian soldier.
I said to him, "Can you do me a favor?
The hospital is a long way from here.
I have trouble seeing,
Everything is dark and confusing.
I cannot see the tunnel."
Then the Captain arrived
He said, "Either you go to the hospital or I will kill you."
With his revolver in his hand, he said,
"Leave or I will shoot you." (53)

I said to him, "I am an Italian
Not an Austrian as you may think
And I am a human being.
And I am proud to tell you this,
And pay attention, Captain, sir,
I am wounded and no one is providing me treatment.
My family is far away
But I have a brother nearby.
For 24 hours, I have been lying on the ground,
Dying of thirst and in excruciating pain."

---

(53) General Luigi Cadorna, Italian Chief of Staff , authorized the executions of over 750 Italian soldiers following trials. Italian officers were known to execute their own men on their own initiative. After Caporetto, the enlisted soldiers were known to have shot some of their officers. Jonathan Shay has written about the importance of ethical behavior by military officers (see foreword, p. xxix).

Sono stato a terra come il cane
E la cera un sergente Calabrese
Il 15 maggio era e si doveva fare
A quel momento portano due austriece
Io col coltello alle mane
E vedo a quelle infame maledette
Assasine mi mise a gridare
Per voi altre la guerra si fece
E l'austriece tutte tremando
Si misero a Dio arecomandando
Allora io arabiando
Sono ferito e nessuno mi sente
Io gettato dentro una fossa di fango
Avete pieta' dei miei lamente
La ferita mi bruciava tanto
Allora viente vicino un tenente
Allora io mormorando
L'officiale ci disse al sergente
Mandamolo allo ospedale
Che lui dice non puo caminare

Tuesday, May 15, 1917

I was on the ground like a dog.
And a Sergeant from Calabria was there
It was May 15th, not yet daylight.
At that moment they brought in two Austrian soldiers.
And I, with a knife in my hand,
Saw those accursed evil ones.
"Assassins," I screamed,
"It is because of you that we are at war."
The Austrians were trembling
And they began praying to God.

At this point, I was enraged.
I am injured and thrown into a muddy ditch.
No one tends to my wounds.
I murmured,
"Have pity, hear my pleas.
My wound feels as if it is on fire,"
A Lieutenant came near me,
And said to the Sergeant,
"Let's send him to the hospital."
The Sergeant replied, "He says he cannot walk."

Allora cera un soldato Siciliano
Sopra le spalle mi vozze mettere
Uscimo fuori e cera un massagraro
Molte lamente e grande gridi
Mi butta a terra senza riparo
Il cannone austrieco si veniva a sentire
Del suo governo che era infamo
Gli Italiani eramo troppo civili
Li prigioniere indietro le vennero a portare
Avevano paura delle miei mane
Io a quattro piede come le animale
Agli Austriace non le venne piu' a vedere
Io con molto coraggio e di scappare
Le cannonate venivano a piovere
Alla protetrice mi mise a pregare
Degli occhi miei mi calavano le vile
Il carso a quel momento era infernale
Io sangue non ce navevo piu' nelle vene
Austriece erano come gli animale
Per forza la guerra dovevano fare

There was a Sicilian soldier nearby.
He put me on his shoulders
We came out of the tunnel and found a massacre.
We could hear moaning and loud screaming.
He threw me to the ground and I had no cover.
We could hear the sounds of Austrian artillery
Firing on orders from their infamous government.
We Italians were too civilized.
The prisoners that were taken behind the lines
Were afraid of my wrath.

I was on my hands and knees like an animal
I could not bear looking at the Austrians any more.
With much boldness, I tried to escape
The onslaught of the artillery that was raining down on us.
I began to pray to the Holy Mother, our Protector,
The cowards were falling before my eyes.
At that moment the Carso was burning.
Blood no longer flowed through my veins. (54)
The Austrians were barbarians
Who, by their nature, had to wage war.

_____

(54) This was said metaphorically but perhaps also in fact as a result of
significant blood loss from his injuries.

Io con molto coraggio e intelligenza
La' vedo con mia sorpresa
Arivo nella trincea di resistenza
Come calava la discesa
Trovo gli amice siciliane
Ci abbracciamo co molta contentezza
Quelli che mi vennero a scavare
Loro con molta alegrezza
Si missero a domandare
Ciccone ora dovemo mangiare
Io ci disse ora vado all'ospedale
Sono ferito alla galeria
Delle 3 taverne si vene a chiamare
E' morta la meta' della compagnia
Io ha voluto Dio mi mi posso salvare
Gli amice miei con molta alegria
La natica destra mi fa male
Sei stato fortunato mi dissero a mia
Disse io amice vi abbraccio mi dare il cuore
Spero mi vi aiuta lo Signore

The Support Trench

With much courage and cleverness,
I reached the support trench. (55)
To my surprise,
As I was climbing down into the trench,
I saw my Sicilian friends.
The soldiers who had rescued me when I was buried alive.
We hugged each other joyfully.
They were happy to see me.
They asked me how I was and said,
"Ciccone, now we have to go eat [celebrate]."

I said to them, "I have to go to the hospital.
I was wounded in the sinkhole,
With the three caves.
Half of my company is dead.
I was saved by the grace of God."
My friends were glad I had survived.
"My right buttock is hurting," I told them.
They said, "You are lucky to be alive."
I responded, "My friends, I embrace you with all my heart.
I pray that God watches over you."

———————————————

(55) WWI trench warfare often involved a complex series of
connecting trenches that served different functions. There were
communication trenches, support trenches, reserve trenches and
etcetera. There was a six-mile-long backup trench system that went
north from Monfalcone to Monte San Michele, a mountain about 900-
feet high (Paolo Pollanzi, personal communication, June, 2014).

O Guerra tu veniste a bestialire
Il Carso e tutto al fuoco del cannone
E' tutto scoperto quanto si vede
Dal Dosso Faite a Monfalcone
Questa e' guerra di morire
Per due infame Imperatore
Di ogni parte agiustava le tire
Pareva scuro e molto calore
l'Austria infama e vendicativa
Il Carso fu la mia rovina
Allora io mi mise a fugire
A quattro piede come l'animale
Era vita che doveva garantire
E per forza potermi salvare
Finalmente venne per sfinire
Arrivo al posto e mi medicaro
Sono ferito per morire
E si apresenta un capitano
E la mi prestaro tutte le cure

The Carso

O' War, you came and transformed us into beasts
The Carso is aflame from artillery fire.
From the Dosso Faite to Monfalcone,
And as far as you can see there is no cover.
This is a war of total death
Caused by two evil Emperors.
From everywhere, the Austrians were adjusting the aim
of their artillery.
The battlefield was dark and very hot.
Infamous and vindictive Austria!
The Carso was my ruin.

Then I began to flee
On my hands and knees like an animal.
My life was at stake,
I had to save myself.
Finally it came to an end;
I arrived at an area where they could treat me.
I was seriously wounded and near death.
A captain approached me.
At last, I was at the field hospital.
There they gave me medical attention.

La subito mi domandaro
Coraggio non avere piu' timore
La cera un cappelano
Lui chiama il dottore
Venite qui' ci disse al capitano
Questo soldato si chiama Ciccone
Coraggio disse il cappellano
Aveva una barba che mi metteva timore
Mi disse te lo bevi un bicchiere di marsala
Allora io molto lo ringraziava
Subito vennero quattro militare
Con la badella prestamente
Alla bulanza mi vennero a portare
Fuggiva di corsa ameatamente
Il cannone ci venne a sparare
Dello sparo non ha fatto niente
A Vallone vozzero fermare
I feriti gridando le lamente
La coscia a me mi faceva male
Ora cera la rotamobile dei militari

There was a chaplain nearby
Who immediately said to me,
"Take heart. You do not have to worry anymore."
He called the doctor.
"Come here," he said to the captain
"This soldier is called Ciccone."
"Courage," said the chaplain,
Who had a formidable beard.
He asked me, "Would you like a glass of marsala?"
I thanked him very much.

Immediately, four soldiers came
With a stretcher
And took me to an ambulance.
We left quickly.
The artillery were firing at us
But the shells did not reach us.
We stopped at the Vallone
Where the wounded were screaming and moaning.
I was in considerable pain from the wound to my thigh
With other soldiers, I was transferred to another ambulance.

Mi misero sopra con molte lamente
Dopo due ore arivo all'ospedale
Mariano il paese si voleva chiamare
La cerano molte serviente
Medice passate Capitane
Sentiva gridare tante agente
Pareva che scannano li maiali
Il Direttore era Calabrese
Doveva essere bruciato dentro la pece
Li medice erano come le carnefice
Gambe e baccia venivano a serrare
E la cerano molte tormente
Di ogni parte si sentiva gridare
Chi chiamava la Vergine potente
Chi S. Giuseppe che le doveva aiutare
Era un ospetale dei morente
0 31 si veniva a chiamare
3 mese ho stato senza avere convaliscenza
La fu destinata la mia sentenza

The Hospital in Mariano

I was in great pain as they put me in the ambulance.
After two hours, we arrived at the hospital
Having experienced many dangers and many problems.
The hospital was located in the town of Mariano. (56)
At the hospital, there were many attendants and
Doctors who were higher in rank than Captain.
I could hear many wounded soldiers screaming.
It sounded like a slaughterhouse.
The Director of the hospital was from Calabria.
He deserved to be burned in pools of boiling pitch. (57)

The doctors were like butchers
They were severing arms and legs, left and right
And there was a mountain of torment.
From throughout the hospital, you could hear screams.
Some called on the Holy Mother
Others were begging Saint Joseph for help.
It was a hospital for the dying.
The hospital was called 0 31.
I was there for three months but did not fully recover.
It was there that I was destined to serve out my sentence.

---

(56) Mariano dei Friuli is a town located in the province of Gorizia and is about 15 miles north of Monfalcone.

(57) In Canto XXII of the *Inferno*, Virgil leads Dante into the Eighth Circle, Fifth Pouch of Hell. Here Dante finds demons tormenting those who abused their power or position to enrich themselves by placing them in boiling pitch:

> All my attention was fixed upon the pitch;
> to observe the people who were boiling in it,
> and the customs and punishment of that ditch.

(Cardi, J. *The Divine Comedy*. New York: W.W. Norton & Company, 1970, p. 114, Canto XXII, Lines 16-18.)

Alle 2 di agosto esco dell'ospedale
La cinquina vozze sigire
Esco del manicomio dei militare
A comando di tappa vozze ire
A Romanz volevo stare
Al Comandante ci venne a dire
Il Reggimento dove stave
Per stasera mettete a dormire
Il 48 lo trove forse domane
Dormo per terra come il cane
La mattina 2 lire mi vennero a dare
Camina dissero prestamente
Il Reggimento e a Civitale
Non sono ore e nemmeno momente
Allora mi metto a camminare
Per la via di Cormos lestamente
Di Mariano veniva a passare
Quello ospedale mi venne a mente
Di quelli assassine mi vene memoria
Vi sto raccontando tutta la storia

I was released from the hospital,
That insane asylum, on August 2nd [1917].
I received five days of pay.
I had to go to the support headquarters
Located in the town of Romans. (58)
I asked the Commanding Officer,
"Where is my Regiment?"
"For tonight just go to sleep
Perhaps tomorrow you will find the 48th." (59)
I slept on the floor like a dog.

Monday, August 6, 1917

In the morning, they gave me two lire
They told me to walk quickly.
The regiment was in Cividale (60)
And there was no time to waste.
So I began walking
Toward Cormons (61) at a fast pace.
Passing through Mariano,
I thought of the hospital.
I remembered those butchers.
I am telling you the whole story.

---

(58) Romans d'Isonzo is a town in the Province of Gorizia in the Friuli
Venezia Giulia region located three miles south of Mariano del Friuli
and is the location of the hospital where Nonno convalesced.

(59) "La Brigata Ferrara," composed of the 47th and 48th Regiments,
took part in the Tenth Battle of the Isonzo.

(60) Cividale del Friuli is a town in the Province of Udine in the Friuli
Venezia Giulia region located in the foothills of the eastern Alps. It is
17 miles north of Romans d'Isonzo.

(61) Cormons is seven miles north of Romans d'Isonzo.

Allora a Carmons venne arrivare
Il treno alle 5 doveva partire
La strada a piedi la debbe a fare
Per causa della agente assassine
A dopo andai a mangiare
Alle 5 si sentiva le gride
Il treno venne arrivare
Io sopra me ne vozze salire
Uscivo dell'Ospedale tutto nervoso
Solo con 5 giorni di riposo
A Udine il treno venne a cambiare
Con tanti pensieri e molti sospiri
Finalmente arrivo a Civitale
Il Reggimento non lo venne a videre
La ho voluto io fermare
Morto di fame e senza bevere
Allora mi mise a domandare
Il comando di tappa dove vole sire
Allora vedo un Capitano e lo salutavo
Il comando subito ci domandavo

I had to get to Cormons.
To catch the train leaving at five p.m.
I had to travel that stretch of road on foot
Because of the agents of destruction.
Later I went to eat.
At five, I heard the announcement,
"The train is arriving."
I went to board the train.
I had left the hospital in a very nervous state
I had only only five days of rest [before being sent back
      into battle].

I was preoccupied and full of dread.
At Udine, (62) I had to change trains.
Finally, I arrived in Cividale. (63)
I did not see my regiment.
I wanted to stop there because
I was very hungry and thirsty.
I started asking,
"Where is the support headquarters?"
I saw a Captain who I saluted and
Quickly asked, "Where is the command?"

---

(62) Udine is a city in northeastern Italy between the Adriatic Sea and the Alps. Udine is 15 miles northwest of Cormons and Cividale is ten miles east of Udine. During World War I, before the Italian defeat in the battle of Caporetto, Udine was the seat of the Italian High Command.

(63) Cividale del Friuli is ten miles north of Cormons.

Mi disse come ti chiami
Ciccone e fui stato nei patimenti
Sono uscito dell'Ospedale
Vai disse a destra disse dolcemente
Il comando di tappa vozze arrivare
La bella citta' era dolente
Che si chiamava Civitale
Sapete dove stanno tale Reggimento
La Brigata Ferrara si veniva a chiamare
Per stasera qua' deve stare
Vedo un Capitano ci disse salutando
Era il 48 e si ebbe a fermare
Io sono stato al comando
Il Reggimento dove stave
Lui mi disse a S. Leonardo
10 cm. distante di quane
Allora io sempre salutando
Lo venne a ringraziare
La mattina la giornata mi vennero a pagare
Eravamo molti militari

La Brigata Ferrara/48th Regiment

He asked me, "What is your name?"
"Ciccone, and I have been through much suffering.
I just got out of the hospital."
He pleasantly told me, "Go to the right
To get to the support headquarters."
The beautiful city of Cividale was suffering.
At the headquarters, I asked,
"Do you know where my regiment can be found?
It is called La Brigata Ferrara [The Ferrara Brigade]. (64)
They told me, "For tonight, you have to stay here."

I saw a Captain from the 48th Regiment [Ferrara Brigade].
I saluted him and he stopped. I said,
"I have been to the support command.
I am looking for the 48th Regiment."
He replied, "It is at S. Leonardo, (65)
Ten kilometers [six miles] to the east."
Always at attention,
I thanked him.
In the morning, they came to pay us.
I was one among many soldiers. (66)

---

(64) The 47th and 48th Regiments make up the Brigata Ferrara. A history of the Ferrara Brigade can be found in *Ufficio Storico del Comando del Corpo di Stato Maggiore, Riassunti storici dei Corpi e Comandi nella guerra 1915-1918.* Volume Terzo. Brigate di Fanteria. Reggio-Ferrara-Parma-Alpi-Umbria-Marche-Abruzzi-Calabria-Sicilia-Cagliari-Valtellina-Palermo-Ancona-Puglie. Volume III. Edited by Ministero della Guerra Ufficio storico, 1926.

The Ferrara Brigade participated in the Eleventh Battle of the Isonzo on the Bainsizza Plateau from August 18 to September 12, 1917. The Italian army was victorious. The Ferrara Brigade took part in the offensive, but as a result of significant causalities (about 1,400 enlisted men and 75 officers), the Brigade was sent behind the front line to regroup. The Twelfth Battle of the Isonzo (Battle of Caporetto) took place from October 24 to November 7, 1917. (Continued)

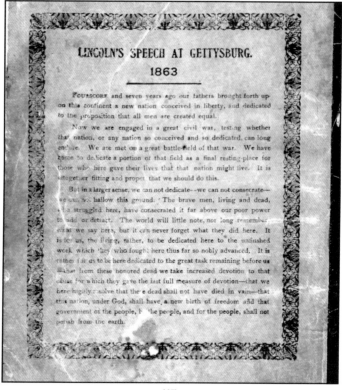

LINCOLN'S SPEECH AT GETTYSBURG.

1863

FOURSCORE and seven years ago our fathers brought forth upon this continent a new nation conceived in liberty, and dedicated
to the proposition that all men are created equal.

Now we are engaged in a great civil war, testing whether
that nation, or any nation so conceived and so dedicated, can long
endure. We are met on a great battle-field of that war. We have
come to dedicate a portion of that field as a final resting place for
those who here gave their lives that that nation might live. It is
altogether fitting and proper that we should do this.

But in a larger sense, we can not dedicate--we can not consecrate--
we can not hallow this ground. The brave men, living and dead,
who struggled here, have consecrated it far above our poor power
to add or detract. The world will little note, nor long remember
what we say here, but it can never forget what they did here. It
is for us, the living, rather, to be dedicated here to the unfinished
work which they who fought here thus far so nobly advanced. It is
rather for us to be here dedicated to the great task remaining before us
--that from these honored dead we take increased devotion to that
cause for which they gave the last full measure of devotion--that we
here highly resolve that the e dead shall not have died in vain--that
this nation, under God, shall have a new birth of freedom and that
government of the people, by the people, and for the people, shall not
perish from the earth.

(67)

---

(64)...On October 27, 1917, the Brigade fought in the area of Purgessimo, between San Leonardo and Cividale del Friuli. The grave situation they found themselves in required that they retreat from that area. The Brigade moved to the Val Chiaro area, three miles north of Cividale. The retreat continued and on October 28th the Brigade arrived at the Tagliamento river, about 35 miles west of Cividale del Friuli. On November 3, 1917 the Brigade crossed the Piave River and arrived in the area of Camposampiero where they began to regroup. World War I finally came to an end a year later on November 11, 1918.

(65) S. Leonardo is about six miles east of Cividale del Friuli and 30 miles north of Monfalcone.

(66) The poem abruptly ends at this point, the last line of the last page of the composition notebook. We believe the poem continues in another composition notebook but this notebook has been lost.

(67) The back cover of the composition notebook.

Photographs

The following photographs were derived from several sources. The pictures of the World War I Memorial Park (WWI MP) and museums located in the Carso and north of Monfalcone were taken on a trip to the Carso battlefield by Natalie and J. Richard Ciccone in June 2014. Paolo Pollanzi guided them to various sites and provided illuminating commentary.

The photographs of Giuseppe Ciccone were provided by Tina Ciccone Sturdevant. She also provided photographs of the Ciccone home in Sant'Eufemia d'Aspromonte and her family from their visit in 1971. The subsequent family photographs were taken during a visit by J. Richard Ciccone's family to Sant'Eufemia in August 1973.

Monument located in the WWI Military Cemetery on the
S. Elia hill, part of the Redipuglia Military Memorial
(WWI MP, June 2014). The inscription reads:
An Unidentified Soldier
Every morning, Mother, and every evening
I hear the echo of your prayer

Trench: WWI trench with soldiers (Image from Museum of the
Third Army, Redipuglia Military Memorial)

Trench: WWI battlefield north of Montfalcone
(WWI MP, June 2014)

Soldiers shooting through holes in trench walls (Image from the
Museum of the Third Army, Redipuglia Military Memorial)

Holes in a protective stone wall
(WWI MP, June 2014)

Close-up of trench with a path between stone trench walls
(WWI MP, June 2014)

Individual walking in a trench
(WWI MP, June 2014)

J. Richard Ciccone and Paolo Pollanzi in one of the trenches
(WWI MP, June 2014)

Nature overtaking a system of connecting trenches
(WWI MP, June 2014)

Museum of Monte San Michele, located on peak three of
Monte San Michele (WWI MP, June 2014)

The insignia of the 680th Section- Machine Gunners
(WWI MP, June 2014)

Direction sign in a trench
(WWI MP, June 2014)

Monument to the Ferrara Brigade on peak three of
Monte San Michele (WWI MP, June 2014)

Monument located on peak three of Monte San Michele to
Italian and Hungarian soldiers (WWI MP, June 2014).
The inscription reads:
On this peak
Italian and Hungarian
Courageous combatants
Became brothers in death

The Redipuglia Military Memorial is located on Monte Sei Busi
in Redipuglia and contains the remains of more than
100,000 Italian soldiers (WWI MP, June 2014)

The uppermost level of the Redipuglia Military
Memorial (WWI MP, June 2014)

WWI Military Cemetery on the S. Elia hill, part of
Redipuglia Military Memorial (WWI MP, June 2014)

WWI Museum: Items found on the battlefield
(Museo Grande Guerra in San Martino del Carso, June 2014)

WWI Museum: Items found on the battlefield
(Museo Grande Guerra in San Martino del Carso, June 2014)

Map of the Isonzo Front (Museum of the Third Army,
Redipuglia Military Memorial, June 2014)

World War I Museum at San Martino del Carso
(June 2014)

Photos of Giuseppe Ciccone
(Years unknown)

Sant'Eufemia d'Aspromonte, Calabria, Italy
(Circa 1976)

Giuseppe Ciccone and Tina Ciccone Sturdevant in front of the
Ciccone home in Sant'Eufemia d'Aspromonte (1971)

Front of Ciccone home in Sant'Eufemia d'Aspromonte
(May 1971)

Back of Ciccone home and entrance to garden
in Sant'Eufemia d'Aspromonte (May 1971)

Tina Ciccone Sturdevant and her four children Gary, Donna,
Lisa and Linda (top) and Giuseppe Ciccone and Francesca Pillari
Ciccone (bottom) in front of Ciccone home (May 1971)

Linda Sturdevant, Giuseppe Ciccone and Tina Ciccone
Sturdevant (top) and Gary Sturdevant (bottom) at the tree that
Garibaldi leaned on when he was wounded in 1862 (May 1971)

Francesca, J. Richard holding Robert, Regina, Giuseppe Ciccone
holding great grandson Louis and Louis Ciccone (August 1973)

J. Richard Ciccone holding Louis, Giuseppe Ciccone
and Louis Ciccone holding Robert (August 1973)

Louis Ciccone, J. Richard holding Robert, Giuseppe, Louis,
Regina, Francesca and Natalie Caputo Ciccone (August 1973)

Louis, Regina, Robert, Giuseppe, Vilma Musacchio Ciccone and
Louis Ciccone in the garden behind the home (August 1973)

Natalie Caputo Ciccone, Robert, Francesca Pillari Ciccone, Regina, J. Richard, Louis and Giuseppe Ciccone (August 1973)

Giuseppe Ciccone with great-grandson Louis Ciccone (August 1973)

In 1968, to mark the 50th anniversary of the end of WWI, the Italian government established the Ordine di Vittorio Veneto with the rank of Cavaliere (Knight) to honor soldiers decorated with the Cross of War (Croce al Merito di Guerre), which was awarded for one year of service in combat operations and being wounded in combat.

Giuseppe Ciccone was made a Knight of the Ordine di Vittorio
Veneto. In this photograph, he is wearing the two medals
presented to him on March 31, 1971 (age 84).

Log of Ferrara Brigade:
August 1 through 6, 1917

Col. Rodolfo Sganga, Military Attaché to the Italian Embassy in Washington D. C., reported that he was unable to access Giuseppe Ciccone's military records. They were lost or destroyed. The search included the military archives and the National Archives in Reggio Calabria.

The Italian Army General Staff Museum provided the Diary of the Ferrara Brigade's 48th Regiment for August and September 1917 (see pp. 113-114 for a brief description of the Ferrara Brigade's participation in the Eleventh and Twelfth Battles of the Isonzo). The following images reproduce the Diary's entries for August 1 through 6, 1917.

Data e giorno della settimana	Dislocazione dei reparti al mattino — Ordini ricevuti e dati — Operazioni eseguite e truppe che vi parteciparono — Stato atmosferico
Venerdì	Il Reggimento svolge una esercitazione tattica con passaggio del ponte sul l'Erbozzo. Tempo bello. Perdite N. N.

Il Colonnello
Comandante del Reggimento

Tarolis

Data e giorno della settimana	
Sabato	Il Reggimento svolge una esercitazione tattica con passaggio del ponte sul l'Erbozzo. Tempo bello. Perdite N. N.

Il Colonnello
Comandante del Reggimento

Tarolis

	N. 143 del Catal.
Data e giorno della settimana	**Dislocazione dei reparti al mattino — Ordini ricevuti e dati — Operazioni eseguite e truppe che vi parteciparono — Stato atmosferico**
5 Domenica	Ha luogo nella mattinata una esercitazione tattica di Brigata. Tempo vario. Perdite. N N
	[timbro] Il Colonnello Comandante del Reggimento *Tarolis*
6 Lunedì	Ha luogo, sotto la direzione del Comandante della Brigata, una esercitazione tattica di Brigata fra Mitana e Monte S. Andrea. (allegato 1) Il Reggimento ha per obbiettivo la conquista delle alture di Monte S. Andrea e stabilirsi sul rovescio delle alture stesse.- La manovra ha inizio alle ore 8 alla presenza di S.E. il Comandante la 2ª Armata Tenente Generale Capello, di S.E. il Comandante del XXVII° Corpo d'Armata Tenente Generale Vanzo e del Comandante la 22ª Divisione Maggior Generale Pacini.- A tale ora una batteria da montagna inizia il tiro di demolizione su tre ordini di trincee situate sulle pendici Sud del Monte S. Andrea; le sezioni lancia torpedini "Bettica" del Reggimento contemporaneamente aprono il fuoco di distruzione dei reticolati antistanti alla prima linea. Alle ore 8.30 l'artiglieria allunga il tiro ed ha inizio lo scatto delle fanterie sotto l'arco della traiettoria. Il V Battaglione effettua il passaggio del ponte sul Torrente Erbezzo, il III. il passaggio a guado del detto Torrente e raggiungono l'obbiettivo prestabilito,

Afterword
Margaret (Maggie) MacAdam
8th grade English class assignment
Twelve Corners Middle School
Brighton, New York

Discovering the Distant:
The Story of J. Richard Ciccone

"The poem helped me discover who he was as a person, what he had been through," my grandfather told me as he recalled translating his own grandfather's poem about his experiences in World War I from Italian to English.

The poem had been passed down to my grandpa from his grandfather's daughter, his aunt. Not knowing much about his reserved grandfather, my great aunt Tina and my grandpa agreed that they wanted to translate it.

He told me this as the two of us sat at the kitchen table, sipping hot chocolate, snow lightly falling outside of the window, even though it was only the middle of October. Every so often, he would get up and go to the dining room, coming back with papers, books, or photo albums to help him tell his story. Each trip seemed to bring more pride and willingness to divulge his story.

My grandpa and his aunt decided it was best to not hire a professional translator but to translate the poem themselves. Although simply paying someone else to do the work would be easier, my grandpa and great aunt took it upon themselves to decipher the poem. "As his daughter and his grandson we were in the best position to give him voice. We thought that we would understand more about him than most others would. Among other things, we also understood the culture that he came from, my grandpa told me. Although they felt it more appropriate to translate the poem themselves, it took years to complete because they had not been trained to translate.

"The effort to translate this poem has been very extensive," my grandpa admits. But when I asked him if the results of the translated poem outweigh his work, he immediately replied, "Oh, no question, it was a labor of love. I loved doing it and I'm very happy to have completed it."

My grandpa was faced with the challenge of how he was not only going to translate the words but how he would translate the poetry aspect. After figuring out that it was a poem when my grandpa first looked at it, and that it also contained a rhyme scheme, he had to decide whether to translate the rhyme scheme or just translate the words. After reading multiple translations of many other poems, my grandpa decided it best to not keep the rhyme in the translation. He did this in order to attempt to preserve his grandfather's voice.

My grandpa's greatest challenge with the translation was dealing with nearly 70 unusual terms. These terms caused great confusion because they were specific to the culture, his grandfather's hometown or, since the poem was about his grandfather's time in the army, military terms. In order to learn the meaning of these terms, my grandpa did numerous things. He received help from the Traversos, friends in Italy. My grandpa also got help with the military words from Col. Rodolfo Sganga at the Italian Embassy in Washington, D.C. My grandparents were also able to visit Italy and see some of the battlefields his grandfather had fought on. While in Italy, their tour guide, Paolo Pollanzi was also able to help with the meanings of some of the terms and even show my grandpa what his grandfather was talking about when he wrote them. Since my grandpa was open to many different people's understanding of the terms, he was able to translate all 70 terms.

Another challenge my grandpa faced is perhaps the greatest challenge of translation: to keep the author's voice and thoughts. When I asked my grandpa who his grandfather was, he answered by pulling out an old photo album from when he and my grandma took my mom and her brothers to Italy when they were kids. As my grandpa recalled the memories, he told me about each picture, including one in which he said it was the only time he had seen his grandfather smile. My grandpa told me, "I hardly knew him because he hardly talked, hardly was around, he was distant."

Barely knowing who his grandfather truly was, my grandpa still had to translate his thoughts into English. Throughout this journey my grandpa had hoped to "get to know him through the poem." With this in mind, my grandpa was able to learn many things about his grandfather, including that he suffered from Post-Traumatic Stress Disorder, or PTSD. My grandpa told me how after knowing this, that "everything began to make sense" and explained a lot about the way his grandfather was after the war.

With his own interest, determination, hard work, and help from others, my grandpa was able to understand his grandfather's life and discover who he was, something he was unable to do while his grandfather was alive. By translating his grandfather's Italian words, soldier actions, and human thoughts, my grandpa was able to discover and build a strong relationship with his distant grandfather, something I am lucky to have with mine.

Bibliography

The following materials (books, monographs, papers, websites and podcasts) were consulted in preparation of this book. Dates in entries refer to the editions consulted, not to first publications.

Ashworth, T. *Trench Warfare, 1914-1918: The Live and Live System.* London: Pan Macmillan Ltd, 2000.

Barthas, L. *Poilu: The World War I Notebooks of Corporal Louis Barthas, Barrel Maker, 1914-1918.* Translated by Edward M. Strauss. New Haven: Yale University Press, 2014.

Binneveld, J.M., Binneveld, H. *From Shell Shock to Combat Stress: A Comparative History of Military Psychiatry.* Leiden: Amsterdam University Press, 1997.

Burgan, M. *The Split History of World War I.* Minnesota: Compass Point Books, 2014.

Buttar, P. *Collision of Empires: The War on the Eastern Front in 1914.* Oxford: Osprey, 2014.

Carlin, D. *Hardcore History: Blueprint for Armageddon.* Podcast.

Cavallaro, G.V. *The Beginning of Futility: Diplomatic, Political, Military and Navel Events on the Austro-Italian Front in the First World War (1914-1917), Volume One.* United States: Xlibris Corporation, 2009.

Clark, C. *The Sleepwalkers: How Europe Went to War in 1914.* New York: Harper Collins, 2013.

Clarke, J.M. Clinical Neurology and Psychiatry: Some Neuroses of the War. *Bristol Medico-Chirurgical Journal.* July, 1916.

Crocq M.A., Crocq L. From shell shock and war neurosis to posttraumatic stress disorder: A history of psychotraumatology. *Dialogues in Clinical Neuroscience,* 2:47-55, 2000.

Faulkner, W. *Requiem for a Nun.* New York: Random

House, 1951.

Fernandez-Mayoralas, A. *The Trench War on the Western Front, 1914-1918.* Madrid: Andrea Press, 2009.

Fiorentino, P. *Sicily through Symbolism and Myth: Gates to Heaven and the Underworld.* Mineola, New York: Legas, 2006.

Follett, K. *Fall of Giants.* Signet: New York, 2012.

Fussell, P. *The Great War and Modern Memory.* Oxford: Oxford University Press, 1975.

Grinker R.R., Spiegel J.P. *Men Under Stress.* New York: McGraw-Hill, 1957.

Groom, W. *A Storm in Flanders: The Ypress Salient, 1914-1918; Tragedy and Triumph on the Western Front.* New York: Atlantic Monthly Press, 2002.

Hart, P. *The Great War: A Combat History of the First World War.* Oxford: Oxford University Press, 2013.

Hastings, M. *Catastrophe 1914: Europe Goes to War.* New York: Alfred A. Knopf, 2013.

Helprin, M. *A Soldier of the Great War.* New York: Harcourt Brace Jovanovich, 1991.

Hemingway, E. *A Farewell to Arms.* New York: Charles Scribner's Sons, 1957.

Horne, A. *The Price of Glory: Verdun 1916.* London: Penguin Books, 1993.

Hughes, G., Blom, P., (Eds.), *Nothing but the Clouds Unchanged: Artists in World War I.* Los Angeles: Getty Research Institute, 2014.

Hughes, R. *The Shock of the New.* Alfred A. Knopf: New York, 1980.

Joll, J. *The Origins of the First World War.* New York: Longman, 1989.

Jones, F.D. *Psychiatric Lessons of War.* In R. Zajtchuk (Ed.), *Textbook of Military Medicine. Part I: Warfare, Weaponry, and the Casualty.* Washington, D.C.: Office of the Surgeon General/Department of the Army, 1991.

Jones, S. *World War I Gas Warfare Tactics and Equipment.* Oxford: Osprey, 1994.

La Grande Guerra: The Italian Front 1915-1918.
Retrieved December 7, 2015, from
www.worldwar1.com

Lussu, E. *A Soldier on the Southern Front.* Translated
by Gregory Conti. New York: Rizzoli, 2014.

Macdonald, J., Cimpric, Z. *Caporetto and the Izonzo
Campaign: The Italian Front 1915-1918.* Great Britain:
Pen and Sword Military, 2011.

Mackay, F. *Asiago, 15/16 June 1918: Battle in the Woods
and Clouds.* South Yorkshire, England: Sword and Pen,
2001.

Mackay, F. *Touring the Italian Front 1917-1918: British,
American, French and German Forces in Northern
Italy.* Southern Yorkshire, England: Pen and Sword,
2007.

MacMillan, M. *The War that Ended Peace: The Road to
1914. New York: R*andom House, 2013.

Moose, G.L. *Fallen Soldiers: Reshaping the Memory of the
World Wars.* Oxford: Oxford University Press, 1990.

Morris, D.J. *The Evil Hours: A Biography of Post-
Traumatic Stress Disorder.* New York: Eamon
Dolan/Houghton Mifflin Harcourt, 2015.

Nicolle, D. *The Italian Army of World War I.* Oxford:
Osprey Press, 2003.

Pols, H. Waking up to shell shock: Psychiatry in the U.S.
military during WWII. *Endeavour.* 30(4):144-9, 2006.

Quarra, A. *La Guerra Italiana nel Primo Conflitto
Mondiale 1915-1918.* Rome: Ugo Pinto, 1965.

Root, G.I. *Battles in the Alps: A History of the Italian Front
of the First World War.* Baltimore: Publish America
2008.

Reynolds, F.J., Taylor, C.W. (Eds). *Collier's New
Photographic History of the World War.* New York:
P.F. Collier and Son, 1918.

Singleton, C.S. *Inferno 2, Commentary.* New
Jersey: Princeton University Press, 1970.

Strachan, H. (Ed.), *The Oxford Illustrated History of the*

First World War. Oxford: Oxford University Press, 2014.

The British Library. Retrieved December 7, 2015 from www.bl.uk

The Great War. Retrieved December 7, 2015, from www. youtube.com/user/TheGreatWar

The Great War: A Photographic Narrative. Holborn, Mark, Ed. London: Jonathan Cape, 2013.

Thompson, M. *The White War: Life and Death on the Italian Front 1915 - 1919.* New York: Basic Books/Perseus Book Group, 2008.

Tuchman, B. *The Guns of August.* New York: MacMillan, 1988.

Ustinova, Y., Cardeña, E. Combat stress disorders and their treatment in ancient Greece. *Psychological Trauma: Theory, Research, Practice, and Policy,* 6(6): 739-748, 2014.

Who's Who - Luigi Cadorna. Retrieved December 7, 2015, from www.firstworldwar.com/bio/cadorna.htm

Yorke, T. *The Trench: Life and Death on the Western Front 1914-1918.* Berkshire, England: Courtside Books, 2014.

La Grande Guerra: The Italian Front 1915-1918. Retrieved December 7, 2015, from www.worldwar1.com